Seventeenth-Century Mother's Advice Books

Seventeenth-Century Mother's Advice Books

Marsha Urban

palgrave
macmillan

SEVENTEENTH-CENTURY MOTHER'S ADVICE BOOKS

First published in 2006 by
PALGRAVE MACMILLAN™
175 Fifth Avenue, New York, N.Y. 10010 and
Houndmills, Basingstoke, Hampshire, England RG21 6XS
Companies and representatives throughout the world.

PALGRAVE MACMILLAN is the global academic imprint of the Palgrave Macmillan division of St. Martin's Press, LLC and of Palgrave Macmillan Ltd. Macmillan® is a registered trademark in the United States, United Kingdom and other countries. Palgrave is a registered trademark in the European Union and other countries.

ISBN 1–4039–7066–1

Library of Congress Cataloging-in-Publication Data is available from the Library of Congress.

A catalogue record for this book is available from the British Library.

Design by Newgen Imaging Systems (P) Ltd., Chennai, India.

First edition: February 2006

10 9 8 7 6 5 4 3 2 1

Printed in the United States of America.

For Millie Lawson

Contents

Illustrations

Appendix

Acknowledgments

I would like to thank the British Library for permission to use their holdings, especially the Brockman Papers, and Phyllis Drake-Brockman for the foresight and generosity to donate her family papers to the library.

I am eternally grateful to Susan Baker who provided emotional support as well as editorial assistance, and I especially thank her for marginal notes on innumerable drafts that provided both guidance and humor in a time when both were truly needed. Thanks, also, to Stefanie Scoppettone for her extremely helpful comments on the last draft. I would also like to thank Eric Rasmussen for helping me find Anne Brockman in the old British Library. Many thanks to Gailmarie Pahmieier, Don Berinati, Liz Swingrover, Ellen Houston, Lorena Stookey, Leann Kumataka, and Merrily Dupree for their sage advice and unselfish support. I am also grateful to Kyle Cassinelli, Carrie Kelley, and Mary Joy Tibay for their help with the appendix.

I want to thank the staff of Palgrave Macmillan for their assistance during the publishing process. I am grateful to Farideh Koohi-Kamali, editor; Lynn Vande Stouwe, assistant editor; and Yasmin Mathew and Elizabeth Sabo, production editors, for supporting both my project and me. Their clear and prompt responses quelled many fears before they became paralyzing. I am also grateful for the work of my copy editor, Rohini Krishnan.

Although Millie Lawson did not live to see this book in any form, guidance at the beginning of my academic life gave me the confidence—against all odds—to venture into graduate school. Thank you, Millie.

Introduction

The seventeenth century was indeed a century of revolution for women writers, whose numbers vastly increased, in conjunction with their rising educational opportunities, the increasing literacy rates, and the changing social and economic conditions.

—James Fitzmaurice and Josephine A. Roberts,
Major Women Writers of Seventeenth-Century England[1]

As a research assistant on the *Hamlet* Variorum project, I was part of a team working at the British Library in the spring of 1996. During breaks from my research, I planned to look for a text written by a Renaissance English woman that I could use as a dissertation topic. I knew the likelihood of finding an undiscovered text was next to nil, but I was hoping that beginner's luck might help. As a new doctoral student and a nontraditional student, my first trip to Europe would certainly present fate with an opportunity. Early in the week, Eric Rasmussen, the lead researcher, found a thin paper report of women's texts in the British Library holdings. Searching through the listing, I wrote down the names of all of the women on the list from the seventeenth and eighteenth centuries. In between working on *Hamlet*, I went to the old manuscript room and poured through the holdings. I can still feel the excitement that I experienced when I first saw the manuscript *Age Rectified*. Here, I believed, was an original, unpublished text of a seventeenth-century woman, and I ordered a microfilm of the text, two poems, and the few letters written by her. I left London confident that my find was a good one.

After months of waiting, the microfilm finally arrived. I ran to the library, closely focusing on each page as the copier transferred the manuscript to paper. In the next few months, I transcribed the text. Although the copies were the best I could get from the microfilm, it was not always easy. Written on both sides of the paper, the ink had seeped through, marring and sometimes obliterating the handwriting on the other side. Additionally, I needed to understand sixteenth- and seventeenth-century handwriting conventions to decipher some of the abbreviations Brockman used.

Once I finished transcribing the text, I began analyzing it for a narrative theory class. Brockman's pragmatic perception of life and her straightforward writing style made the treatise interesting. Although Brockman wrote *Age Rectified* in 1709, she was fifty-one when she wrote, therefore, she was a product of the seventeenth century. Based on my assumption that *Age Rectified* had never been published, I analyzed the ethos and persona of the text written for a much smaller audience—a manuscript, rather than a publication audience. A few months later, I found the printed version in the ESTC collection of microfilms—I was devastated.

The discovery of the printed text forced me to revisit the British Library on my own the following year. I began the tedious job of searching through listings and manuscripts for another woman of a similar background, but I never forgot Brockman. One day while reordering other manuscripts to inspect, I also ordered Brockman's *Age Rectified.* Although the text was a copy, something kept bringing me back to it. While thumbing through her manuscript I noticed marginal notation like signatures and small dashes. Why were signatures copied? It made no sense. Looking through the whole manuscript, areas of it began to pop out at me. Signatures and short dashes in the margins were odd for a hand-copied text. I ordered the printed text and compared the two—the short dashes appeared in the margins of the manuscript at the precise spot of page breaks in the printed text. Although I had seen the corrections before, I never noticed that many of these were in another handwriting. I sat back and pondered the evidence. How did this fit in with Lady Anne Brockman? What if this was not a copy but a draft of the printed text—"Aha." That made sense, but could I prove it?

Returning to Reno, I began to research printing practices. I found evidence that authors often gave printers their handwritten manuscript to set the printed text. The printer made check marks on the manuscript, much like the ones I found in the Brockman manuscript, when pages were completed. Additionally, they marked signatures on the manuscript to keep track of the printing and to keep the printing organized. Further research in common copying mistakes showed that at least one of the sentence level corrections was actually editing. Although the marginal notes made a good argument for a draft, another point against Brockman as a copier was her background as a gentlewoman. She could afford to buy the book and her husband traveled to London, so he could have purchased it there. Printer's marks, Brockman's affluence, and editorial corrections assured me that I had an original manuscript, and hence I attributed the author as Lady Anne Brockman. Now that I completed an attribution of authorship, I had to test my argument.

Susan Baker, my committee chair, was my first help in establishing proof. When I presented the argument to her, she assured me that I had, indeed, proven authorship, but the argument needed further testing. I presented my findings at a women's conference in Reno, and they agreed with my findings. I then made a presentation at the Rocky Mountain Modern Language Association Conference in a Renaissance literature session. The five specialists in the field who attended the presentation approved my attribution of Brockman as author. Now, I needed to look at Brockman in the broader context of the genre, mother's advice books.

Until recently, comparatively little has been written about mother's advice books of the seventeenth century. The republication of these books in twentieth-century anthologies will, no doubt, change that. Selections and full texts of mother's advice books can now be found in widely accessible anthologies such as *The Longman Anthology of Women's Literature* (2000), Randall Martin's *Women Writers in Renaissance England* (1996), and Sylvia Brown's *Women's Writing in Stuart England* (1999). These expanded anthologies allow access to women's writing that were previously denied to a much larger audience—undergraduates, postgraduates, and a general audience interested in women's writing, but who do not have access to manuscripts or Wing Catalog microfilms and ESTC microfilm collections. Additionally, recent full editions, such as Betty S. Travitisky's *The Early Modern Englishwoman: A Facsimile Library of Essential Works, Series I, Printed Writings, 1500–1640: Part 2, Volume 8, Mother's Advice Books*, and Jean Le Drew Metcalfe's edition of *The Mothers Legacy to her Vnborn Childe* (2000), also spur interest in the genre. These publications include the popular published works by Elizabeth Grymeston, Dorothy Leigh, Elizabeth Clinton, Elizabeth Josceline, and Elizabeth Richardson but little else. Until now, no other mother's advice books have been reclaimed and republished.

This book uncovers a previously ignored mother's advice book—*Age Rectified*. Published in 1709, this advice book is a unique addition to the genre. While most of the popular mother's advice books address children in a didactic and pious manner, *Age Rectified* addresses mothers, and more specifically, aging mothers, in a tone that is far more pragmatic than pious. The printed texts of the popular mother's advice books proudly declare the names of the authors on the title pages and delineate the author's heritage and life circumstances in the introduction. The title page of *Age Rectified* contains only a hint of the author, "one of the same sex." In the past, this "hint" would be enough to identify the author as female, but as much recent scholarship demonstrates, not all texts that attribute authorship to a woman were actually written by women. Men obscured their identities in an effort to publish and sell both the male and female versions of their advice books, and many battles of the pamphlet wars came from the same hand.[2] *The Mothers Counsell, or, Live within Compasse* (1630) by M. R., which has recently been revealed as authored by a male, is one such text that strove to be labeled women's writing. *Age Rectified*, however, can be proven as a text written by a woman—Lady Anne Brockman.

Unlike authors of other mother's advice books, Brockman uses the role of mother to rear her children in a way that preserves love for their mother, rather than prioritizing love for God. These loving children then take up their roles as caretakers, especially of their widowed mothers, and responsible adults within the family structure. Brockman advises mothers to provide moral lessons with a firm but loving hand, so children can be taught respect for, love of, and care for their aging mothers—"to make reciprocal Indearments betwixt Parents and Children."[3] Additionally, Brockman reminds mothers that as children grow to adulthood, the mother/child relationship should grow with them. She reminds women that their children need financial stability, a moral base, and mutual respect, in addition to open communication between parent and child. The mother/child relationship spans a continuum of caretaker positions. As the ravages of time and the expectations of society deplete the power of the parent, they simultaneously build the authority of the offspring, effectively shifting the caretaker role from mother/child to child/mother.

This book presents the results of scholarly inquiry, highlighting the essentials of the investingation. Chapter 1 discusses seventeenth-century mother's advice books and provides background on some of the topics that were important to seventeenth-century Englishwomen. Although publishing was usually a venue closed to women, motherhood seems to have provided a loophole to the social rule. In fact, authors of mother's advice books entered publishing through their private roles as mothers, who, unlike women in general, cannot be forced to remain silent if their entry into publication is to help their children and all children by doing so. A discussion of the most popular mother's advice books of the time demonstrates that most authors of this genre were middle-class women who were afraid they would die before their children became adults. The pious tenor of all the mother's advice books of this period permeates the texts. All of the mother's advice books are didactic and religious—and all endorse and enact self-sacrifice.

A discussion of mothers and older women, how they were viewed in society, and why some of those viewpoints existed is needed to understand Brockman and her text. Although her primary audience would have been members of the middle to upper classes, this chapter's discussion about older women covers all situations. The physical changes of aging signal not only an entry into a new stage of life—old age—but also a change in social standing. Declining physical and mental abilities often accompanied, and sometimes caused, a decline in financial standing. Such changes affected nearly every part of the life of the elderly, and as one of the gentry whose large estates often contained multigenerational households, Brockman knew that this often forced women to live with their adult children.[4] Similarly important for familial relationships is attitude. Age often brings an attitude of prerogative mitigated by wisdom, experience, and longevity, which can either be revered or repulsed. Brockman suggests strategies women could use to be accepted by and live with their adult children without great difficulties. If, however, the locale of Brockman's advice is moved from a private estate to a larger community, then the advice could be good strategies for other women. They, too, can be accepted by and live peaceably within their multigenerational communities. Chapter 1 also includes demographic information: life expectancy rates, childbirth mortality rates, breast-feeding, and the population of gentry in England, especially Kent. Setting the scene of seventeenth- and early eighteenth-century England, the chapter explains something of the daily life and concerns of women of that time—women like Anne Brockman. This information gives the cultural background for the following chapter that discusses the major mother's advice books and *Age Rectified*.

Although little is known about Lady Anne Brockman, some facts are available and more information has been culled from a few letters found in the Brockman Papers at the British Library. Coupled with a general knowledge of the era's gentry, particularly women, a portrait emerges of Brockman as an intelligent, authoritative, and gifted woman who could easily have written an advice book. Her authority as a gentlewoman permeates her letters and her advice. In her roles of mother, wife, and mistress of a large estate, Brockman gives advice as easily as she gives household orders. Chapter 2 discusses Brockman and her publication, *Age Rectified*. As might be expected, her advice book deviates from the earlier books in theme, style, and intended audience. Brockman's audience is mothers, rather than children. Her theme is old age and the strategies that can ensure happiness while living with adult children. Her style is secular and self-serving. Many of Brockman's ideas concerning child rearing mirror those of John Locke. In *Some Thoughts Concerning Education*, Locke advises parents on how to raise their male children. He is speaking from his own experiences and observations, rather than fatherhood. Although rearing her children well is important to Brockman, it is not only for their benefit, but also for hers. Brockman's advice places the role of a mother in a whole new light.

Chapter 3 attributes the authorship of the printed text (*Age Rectified*) to Brockman based on textual evidence. Brockman's ability to write is supplemented with an extensive examination of the marginal notes of the holograph, "Age Rectified." This research supplies ample evidence to establish Brockman as the author of the text by proving that the marginal notes are those of a compiler and/or printer. Together, the evidence points to the only possible author—Lady Anne Brockman. The edition of the printed text of *Age Rectified* and a facsimile of the Brockman manuscript are formatted on facing pages. The layout of this edition allows comparison of the two texts.

The special case of Lady Anne Brockman's *Age Rectified* needs to be seen in the context of mother's advice books, attitudes toward older women in her period, biographical information about Brockman herself, and the text she wrote and published. Together, these chapters provide a portrait of an English gentlewoman—confident in her position and able to advise other women—who ventured into publishing to secure a safe haven and happy life for aging women. Although as a whole, the texual and biographical evidence attributes authorship to Brockman, it also emphasizes the need for continued research in the field. The Brockman case demonstrates there are more women writers to be found in archival libraries, parish records, attics, government records, and myriad dusty boxes.

The appendix contains facsimiles of Brockman's letters and poetry and her mother's, Anne Glydd, handwritten family history. These manuscripts highlight the personal and familial aspects of Brockman's life. The short, but telling, history of Glydd's children and grandchildren testifies to the fear parents and grandparents felt concerning the survival of their children. Glydd's entries at the birth of her grandchildren include a prayer for their longevity—pleading with God, she asks for long lives for her grandchildren and promises they will be good Christians throughout their lives. Facsimiles, especially in our visual society, allows the reader to "see" beyond the words, to experience the rise and fall of hand strokes, the archaic spelling, and capitalization—the visual textualization of the past. Together, the manuscripts and the discussions of the genre of mother's advice books, the society of seventeenth-century England, and the authorship of *Age Rectified* provide a source book of how the past is recreated from the perspective of the present.

* * *

Notes on Textual and Editorial Policy

The decision about the degree of modernization of the text takes into account accessibility to a wide audience versus an awareness of the text's historical difference. Fully modernizing the text for spelling, punctuation, capitalization, and font can conceal the historical distance between the traditional text and the contemporary text, inadvertently inviting the reader to evaluate the text through a modern lens. For this reason, I have chosen to make minimal editorial changes in an attempt to remind the reader of the text's antiquity. The original spelling and abbreviations have been retained. Punctuation (apostrophes, capitalization, and italicization) and paragraphing have been retained. Endnotes supply a gloss for words whose meanings have changed over time as well as contextual information when necessary. The abbreviation "&" has been expanded to "and." The copy text for this edition is the first English edition published in 1709.

1

Mothers, Wives, Widows, and Mother's Advice Books of the Seventeenth Century

Seventeenth-Century English Women

Women of late seventeenth- and early eighteenth-century England experienced a world where one woman could rule the country, but women, in general, had almost no legal power of their own. Women were in the same legal category as children, wards, lunatics, idiots, and outlaws. The ideal of woman dictated chastity, modesty, and silence. Moreover, this ideal placed women almost solely within the domestic sphere, hence many believed women did not need an extensive education. Women's domestic education and the societal expectation of silence negatively impacted women's ability to publish. Men, then, frequently wrote for and to women. Men wrote cookbooks and midwifery books, and they even put together most of the first needlework books.[1] Although men could, and often did, give women advice about motherly topics, they could never experience motherhood. The exclusively female functions of childbirth and breast-feeding united women as mothers. This role gave women a natural authority that men could only imagine. Through their function as mothers, the authors of mother's advice books entered publishing to advise their children and other women to live a good life. Their environment included childbirth, breast-feeding, illness and death, family, class, and aging. Although the authors wrote about domestic topics, only Anne Brockman advised women about their future: old age.

Life Expectancy

The estimated average life expectancy at birth for late sixteenth-/early seventeenth-century English citizens varied according to their social status, geographic location, diet, genes, work, and gender. Although Lawrence Stone estimates life expectancy for the general population to be 52 or 53 years,[2] a more recent estimation by Edward Wrigley and Roger Schofield approximate it at just under 39.7 years,[3] whereas Keith Wrightson estimates life expectancy to be as low as 33 years.[4] Anyone who lived past childhood increased their prospect of a longer life, since infant and child mortality rates were extremely high. In *Observations* from 1662, John Graunt estimated that 36 percent of Londoners died before the age of 6.[5] More recent scholarship estimates that one-quarter of all children born during the period of 1550–1649 would not live to the age of 10.[6] For the general population, the secret to a long life during this time period was to reach the age of 30, and those who did could expect to live to the ripe old age of 59. The advantages of wealth, better diets (better food and more of it), and less strenuous labor combined to increase the life expectancy of men who ranked as squires and above. After 1570, heirs of the wealthy who survived until the age of 21 could expect to live into their early sixties.[7]

Geography and socioeconomic status affected life expectancy. In London, crowding (which increased disease and accidents), poor sanitation, and a general increased likelihood of disease all took their toll on the population, regardless of social status. The higher risk to Londoners affected everyone who lived there, but it was most detrimental to the poor. Roger Finlay explains,

> Expectation of life at birth varied greatly from the wealthy to poorer parishes of London. St. Peter Cornhill [a prosperous parish], 1580–1650 had an expectation of life of thirty-four to thirty-six years. Comparatively, the poor parish of St. Mary Somerset, 1606–1653, had a life expectancy at birth of only twenty-one years.[8]

In addition to better diet, less physical labor, and less hazardous work, the wealthy inhabitants of London lived in larger houses, used carriages rather than walking in streets strewn with sewage and increased hazards by accident, visited private parks, and made trips into the country during the summer. Stone calculated that of the 243 peers alive in England between 1558 and 1641, 42 percent (103), died in their fifties

Figure 1.1 Life Expectancy of Peers, 1558–1641 based on Expectations of Life at 21 of Heirs of Squires and Above. Lawrence Stone. *The Family, Sex and Marriage; in England 1500–1800*. New York: Harper & Row, Publishers, 1977, 72.

and sixties, but 13.5 percent (33), survived into their seventies, and about 6 percent (15) into their eighties (see figure 1.1).[9] Unfortunately, there are not any such records known to exist about the poor. Although some of the poor lived into their eighties, they were an anomaly.

The estimation of life expectancy, especially in earlier research, is often given for the whole population, rather than subdivided into male and female.[10] Recent research estimates women's life expectancy was on average two years longer than that of men.[11] Poverty and childbirth affected women's longevity, but men tended to be more prone to disease, and periodically, war. In both genders, though, life expectancy increased for those who lived past the age of thirty. Women were four times more likely to die in the first ten years of marriage than men and twice as likely in the second ten years. Once they survived twenty years of marriage—and childbirth—they were more likely to survive to old age than men. If a woman lived into her early forties, she probably would live into her sixties.[12] A survey of the Salisbury census in 1625 "produced in one parish a woman of a hundred, another of ninety-nine, five women in their eighties, a married couple consisting of a man of ninety-nine and his fifty-year-old wife and seven men over eighty."[13] In 1695, it is estimated that 5 percent of the population of Linchfield was over the age of sixty.[14] Whether male or female, people over the age of sixty were considered very old or elderly—much like those over seventy or eighty in the twenty-first century.

Childbirth Mortality Rates

Every stage of childbirth exposed women to physical discomfort and the possibility of death. Even uncomplicated births subjected the mother to sharp discomfort and pain, as well as lingering distress. For some part of the nine months, the seventeenth-century mother, like the twenty-first-century mother, could experience varying degrees of back pain, stomach disorders, leg swelling, exhaustion, and bladder frequency, but in the seventeenth century there was precious little to alleviate or minimize these problems. Lawrence Stone states,

> For women, childbirth was a very dangerous experience, for midwives were ignorant and ill-trained, and often horribly botched the job, while the lack of hygienic precautions meant that puerperal fever was a frequent sequel. All too common were such stories as one recorded succinctly by Oliver Heywood in 1684:
>
> "Mistress Earnshcaw of York was in sore labour, had her child pulled from her by piecemeal, died at last, left a sad husband."[15]

Stone considers the childbirth mortality rate high, although he does not state a number. Many scholars now consider Stone's estimation, based on upper- and middle-class narrative, an exaggeration because of the chosen population. Since this population had more children per person, the percentage of death in childbirth would be higher as well. In 1616, Frenchman Jacques Guillemeau asserted that "of a thousand births, there is scarce one found that is amiss."[16] His estimation of 1 per 1,000 seems a bit low considering the medical technology of the seventeenth century. Modern calculations for childbirth mortality rates for the seventeenth century vary, but all agree that most pregnancies were, on the whole, uncomplicated:

- Roger Schofield suggests 9.3 per 1,000 or less than 1 percent of mothers died in childbirth in Elizabethan England.
- English mortality rates worsened during the reign of Charles II to 15.7 per 1,000 or about 1.5 percent.[17]
- By 1657–1688, Schofield estimates 21 in 1,000 or 2 percent of women died in childbirth, 14.5 per 1,000 in 1700–1749 or 1.5 percent.[18]
- Lucinda McCray Beier cites 106 women who died in childbirth in 1648, 213 in 1652, and 194 in 1660, but does not have the figures for the number of births during these periods.[19]
- Sara Mendelson and Patricia Crawford estimate childbirth mortality rates during 1550–1720 at 6 to 7 percent.[20]

In comparison, childbirth mortality rates in the United States in 2000 were 0.1 per 1,000 or less than one-tenth of a percent.[21] In comparison, Sierra Leone, a third world country in sub-Saharan Africa whose general medical technology is more on the par of seventeenth-century England, has a childbirth mortality rate that comes much closer to some of the estimates of seventeenth-century England; the rate for 1997 was 1,800 per 100,000 or 1.8 percent.[22]

Although childbirth mortality rates were higher in the seventeenth century than in the modern United States, they were significantly lower than people have usually assumed. If death in childbirth was much rarer in reality than in the fears of pregnant women, why then were women and their families so afraid of death during childbirth? The fear could be based on the practical issues of the family; the death of a mother in childbirth caused major difficulties for the surviving family members. Although the mortality rates were lower in actuality than in perception, the exaggerated fear of death in childbirth may have arisen, in part, from the undeniable fact that childbirth would disrupt a household. First, if the infant survived the mother, a wet nurse was needed to feed the infant—a huge expense. Second, if there were other children, they had to be cared for in addition to the infant. As there were no life insurance policies and day care centers to provide money or assistance with the newborn and/or other children, the financial disruption could be cataclysmic.

Scholars generally overestimated mortality rates in childbirth until recent studies included the poor. Until then, most of the information about childbirth came from diaries of middle- and upper-class women and men. Dorothy McLaren points out a class difference in the childbirth rate: "[T]here is no doubt that the fertility of wealthy women between 1570–1720 was often appallingly high. It was not uncommon for a wealthy woman to bear twenty children."[23] Since most of the written records in existence come from the upper classes, the perception of the high mortality rate came from them as well. Elizabeth Josceline wrote her mother's advice book because she believed, and rightly so, that she would die in childbirth. This text was published and republished, emphasizing high mortality rates by its example. Diaries of both men and women of the upper classes expressed concern about death during childbirth. Since the birth rate of the rich was much higher than for the poor, the mortality rate in childbirth would be as well—thus the heightened fear. Repeated pregnancies could be a strain on the mother's health as well as be a factor that increases the probability of death in childbirth. The availability of written records of the upper classes about this fear gave scholars a skewed perception of the danger.

To help women through pregnancy, herbal medicine offered a variety of remedies.[24] Herbal medicine yielded an assortment of salves and elixirs to hasten and ease delivery. These remedies can be found in private recipe and remedy books, including in that of Anne Glydd, Anne Brockman's mother. In addition to herbal remedies, devotional exercises provided women with some relief. "Though framed by reference to Eve's transgression, their prayers did not dwell on pain and punishment, but stressed instead the blessings of fruitfulness, honor to women, divine deliverance and the prospect of salvation."[25] By stressing the blessing of childbirth, religious leaders such as Calvinist clerics bestowed upon women and their roles as mothers a duty ordained by God. Certainly, prayer can placate fear, which in turn, can relieve stress, thus calming the pregnant woman and possibly making the pregnancy easier. In the twenty-first century, stress is the enemy of all—affecting the physical as well as the emotional health. Mantras and prayers help relieve some stress and take the focus away from pain. In the seventeenth century, the blessings of and prayers by the mother could often diminish the pain and the fears.

Breast-feeding

The phenomenon of wet nurses occurred primarily in the middle and upper classes in seventeenth-century England. Most of the mothers of lower socioeconomic classes had to breast-feed their own children, because they could not afford to hire wet nurses. During the twentieth century, reliable baby formulas enabled women to feed their children using bottles, rather than breasts, and wet nurses were no longer needed because even women of lower socioeconomic strata could afford formula. Some seventeenth-century urban women with more income and parish connections understood the negative effects of city air on children. When they could afford to, they sent their infants to a wet nurse, and they sent them to one in the county. "Parishes around London hosted large numbers of city infants."[26] Medical necessity also forced women to have a wet nurse. When a mother produced too little milk or had problems with her nipples cracking or becoming unbearably painful, she had to find a wet nurse for her child's survival.

Although finances forced most women of the lower classes to breast-feed, the ability to pay a wet nurse was not the sole reason why wealthy women did not breast-feed their children. Other pressures exerted on wealthy women forced them to hand their infants over to strangers for two or three years. The need to produce male heirs, the high child mortality rates, the contraceptive effects of lactation, and the perceived affects on the appearance of the woman were the main reasons wealthy women did not breast-feed.[27] In patriarchal societies, titles and lands are inherited through the males of the family. Although females can inherit, many essentials of the family are lost when this happens. As heiresses marry, assuming they marry into their own class, the estates of their husbands become their homes. Such was the case of Anne (Glydd) Brockman; she married William Brockman and lived on his estate, Beachborough. When her mother died, the Glydd estate, Pendhill, was sold, and the family name lost. Moreover, when offspring remained unmarried and childless, they became the last in their line. If there were no direct family members to inherit, the title and estate were often given to cousins; if the cousin had another last name, it could be joined with the benefactor's name. In the case of the childless James Brockman, Anne Brockman's last surviving son, he bequeathed his estate to his cousin, Ralph Drake. This inheritance, though, came with a name change. Ralph Drake's family name altered from the time of the inheritance. Although neither family name was lost, from that point on Ralph Drake became Ralph Drake-Brockman, the family name became Drake-Brockman and was passed down from generation to generation. To guarantee against the loss of the family name, women had to undertake producing and rearing male offspring. Wealthy women insured against the high childhood mortality rate by having more children—often ten or more. Anne Brockman was one of eight children, and she was the only offspring at her mother's funeral. By having such a large number of children, wealthy families hedged their familial bets against childhood mortality rates.

In addition to the essentials of the inheritance problem, women were also advised against breast-feeding, because it was believed that breast-feeding would ruin their physical attractiveness. This belief, no doubt, was reinforced by the haggard appearance of poor women who breast-fed their children. Considering malnutrition and the physically strenuous work experienced by the poor, they would have aged much faster than the well-fed and well-rested upper-class women, even if they had not breast-fed their children. Moreover, the belief that sexual intercourse corrupted the milk became a more immediate danger—especially to inheritances. Many medical books advised against intercourse during the period in which women breast-fed their child, and breast-feeding usually lasted well over a year. David Cressy discusses general theories concerning lactation: "humoral theory on the circulation and conservation of fluids associated milk with blood, and lactation with menstruation."[28] Many physicians followed Aristotle's belief that woman's milk was nothing more than blood made white in the breasts. John Sadler, 1636, observed that "so long as the woman giveth such to the child, and hath store of milk in her breasts, her terms be of little or no quantity . . . forasmuch as ebbing of the one is the flowing of the other."[29] The main religious groups, Catholic and Protestant, also discussed the matter of sex during the period of breast-feeding. Catholics reminded women their first duty was to their husband, and this duty included conjugal rights.[30] Many theologians concluded that conjugal duties came before maternal duties. Protestant preachers considered maternity the ultimate role for a woman, and advised men to accept their loss of sleep to allow their wives to fulfill their maternal duties.[31] Many husbands demanded their conjugal rights, and rather than corrupting their child's food supply, they made the decision to hire a wet nurse.[32]

In addition to the transformation of blood to milk, many believed breast milk transferred the mother's good qualities to her child.[33] Even though good qualities were inherent in the milk, caution in the beginning was needed. Many experts of the time believed colostrum, a yellow fluid high in protein and immune factors secreted by the mammary glands in the first few days after birth, was harmful. Eucharius Roesslin advised,

> it shall be that the child suck not of the mother's breast by and by as soon as it is born, but rather of some other woman's for a day or two, for because the cream, as they call it, straight after birth, the first day in all women doth thicken and congeal.[34]

Containing immune factors, colostrum is not harmful, but healthy. If a wealthy woman took this advice to allow another woman to breast-feed her infant in the first few days, then she was actually exposing the infant to diseases by wasting natural immune factors. Again, most poor women did not have the luxury of a wet nurse, even in the first few days following birth, so their children did receive immune factors, making them more resistant to disease. Although there are no studies that prove breast-fed children of the poor were healthier than the wealthy children with wet nurses, people did notice and write about the differences. In 1671, Jane Sharpe, a well-known and well-published mid-wife, explained that, "the usual way for rich people is to put forth their children to nurse, but that is a remedy that needs remedy . . . because it changeth the natural disposition of the child, and oftentimes exposeth the infant to many hasards."[35] Sharpe could not have known about immune factor, but many noticed the difference between infants of the poor and those of the wealthy. In his pamphlet *The Compleat Mother*, Henry Newcome railed,

> Children of our nobility and gentry . . . in their infancy generally are more unhappy than the sons of country peasants. The poor tenant's child is for the most part nursed in its own mother's bosom, and cherished by her breasts, whilst the landlord's heir is turned out, exiled from his mother's embraces as soon as from her womb, and assigned to the care of some stranger.[36]

In addition to the loss of physical protection by employing a wet nurse, psychological protection—the bonding between mother and child during breast-feeding—is also lost. Although the suppression of the flow of milk enabled women to produce offspring annually, giving children over to a wet nurse may have stymied the mother's maternal instinct. Additionally, the lack of bonding at the mother's breast may impact the attitude of the child to its mother. Further, Wiesner suggests with regard to the psychological damages that, "because of the separation from the wet nurse when weaned, it can be seen as contributing to the negative ideas about women, particularly fickleness and changeability."[37] This possible psychological damage may help account for the prevalence of fickle and inconstant women in sixteenth- and seventeenth-literature, since most literary authors were men from the middle and upper classes. There has not been any research regarding this possibility, and it is questionable whether this link can be seen as more than an interesting theory. After all, texts before and after the wholesale use of wet nurses contained fickle and inconstant women. Moreover, no studies have been undertaken concerning which authors were breast-fed by their mothers and which were not.

Once the decision was made to hire a wet nurse, the choice of the wet nurse was crucial. Jane Sharpe suggested the finest milk came from a nurse "of sanguine complexion . . . not a woman that is crooked, or squint-eyed, nor with a misshapen nose or body, or with black ill-favored teeth or with stinking breath, or with any notable depravation."[38] A ruddy complexion implies health, and black teeth, bad breath, and misshapen nose can imply ill health as well, all justifiable physical signs of an unhealthy person. The rejection of the squint-eyed and misshapen body, though, may not correlate directly with health, but with the belief that imperfect bodies reflect sin. Once an acceptable wet nurse was chosen, she had to be compensated. It was not cheap to hire wet nurses. The account paid for Katherine Poulett in 1650 for eighteen months was thirty pounds. This did not include extras such as rent, clothing, and presents of all kinds that were often part of the deal.[39] Research estimates a maidservant was paid thirty-nine shillings a year or fifty-nine shillings for eighteen months, but only after working for three years. A shilling was worth one-twentieth of a pound; Poulett was paid twenty pounds a year or four hundred shillings—a much more lucrative proposition. Feeding the future master was much more profitable to a woman than caring for the present master.

Wealthy families, by employing a wet nurse, should have guaranteed an heir by increasing the number of children born. Unfortunately, it may have had the opposite effect. By using a wet nurse, wealthy couples exposed their infants to diseases without protection of natural immune factors from the mother, lessened the psychological bond between mother and child, exposed the infant to possible "bad" homes and a hired wet nurse who might not have the emotional investment of a mother. It is no wonder people like Jane Sharpe noticed that poor families had healthier and happier children than those who lived with wet nurses.

Gentry

In the accepted social strata, the gentry occupy the level below nobility, but above the yeoman class. The gentry consisted of lesser nobility, gentlemen, Baron/Baronet ("Sir," wife called "Dame," often called "Lady" by courtesy), Knight, Esquire, Gentleman, and Clergyman—in that order.[40] The gentry lived on and for their estates. For this reason, their households revolved around maintaining and expanding the family and the estate, not creating independent households. This perpetuation of inheritance changed the household. Adult brothers and sisters, uncles and aunts, and other relations were often housed at the family home.[41] Thus, the gentry of Kent, 2 to 3 percent of the whole population, often lived in multigenerational households. In the northern upperlands, inheritances were commonly made whereby one child bought the land left to the others to preserve the estate and provide for the younger children. Wrightson adds that "more generally younger children were provided for by an allocation of portions of household goods, farm stock, and cash legacies." Even though the gentry focused on saving their estates, turnover at the lower edges of gentility occurred. In Kent, for example, there were 763 gentle families in 1600, 774 in 1642, and 662 in 1695.[42]

Gentle families were only 2 percent of the population of Kent and Lancashire in the early seventeenth century, and the percentage was about the same across the nation, but these families controlled a large portion of the nation's wealth. In the mid-seventeenth century, 50 percent of English land was owned by the gentry.[43] The gentry also had larger families than the average English family. Based on the curate of Gooodnesome-next-Wingham, Laslett lists mean household size and individual numbers of persons and kin in English households. Less than 5 percent of the families were gentry, but nearly 10 percent of the number of people were gentry. The gentry had 8 percent of the children or 2.33 children per family, while the other classes had 1.8 children per family. Poor families had an average of .92 children. The gentry, then, had 30 percent more children per family than all the lower classes, and nearly 250 percent more children per family than the poor. The average size of the gentry's household was nine, and the average number of servants per household was five or nearly two servants per family member. Of the other families who had servants, they had, on average, one servant per family. Ninety-six percent of the families were below the status of gentry. The largest family (22) was part of the gentry; tradesmen and poor men had the smallest size family at one each.[44] Of the 1,349,586 families in England in 1688, 800 were baronets (.06 percent), and their yearly income per family was £800.[45] For the most part, the gentry married within the gentle society of their counties. In insular Kent, 82 percent of marriages in the gentry were between two gentry.[46] Laslett also estimated the mean average age at which people married for the Diocese of Canterbury during the period 1619–1660. The average marriage age for gentry was 26.18 years for men and 21.75 years for women.[47]

Kent

The Folkstone-Hythe area of Kent, where Anne Brockman spent her married life, had about 30–35 inhabitants per square mile.[48] Families of the gentry comprised about 2 to 3 percent of the rural population, and their incomes ranged from about £10,000 a year to about £200 a year. The foundation of the landed wealth was careful estate management through successive generations and the investment of the surplus from rents into prudent purchases of new lands. Financial management was essential for keeping and increasing an estate, but the gentry also owed part of their wealth to fortunate marriages.[49] Sir William Brockman's marriage to Anne Glydd, heiress, was one such fortunate marriage, combining her inheritance with that of the Brockmans to form an even stronger financial base. The arrangement of financial security and social position brought together two important English families. The continuation of the Brockman family rested on another marriage, two distant relatives from both sides of the family. When James Brockman died childless, he had to guarantee the continuation of the family name and the estate. He, like the childless Elizabeth I, found this continuity in his cousins.

The gentry did own 50 percent of English lands, but as learned gentlemen, they were also expected to serve their counties. The gentry filled the positions of justices for the county, which Chalklin points out required time: "At least between 1642 and 1689 the justices met only twice annually in formal session at Maidstone or Canterbury, in most cases according as to whether they lived in west or east Kent, and they were also expected to appear before the judges during the Assizes at Maidstone." The bulk of civic duty for the gentry was done in their own district. In addition to justices, the duties of a Member of Parliament involved fewer gentlemen for a service that was spasmodic and seasonal. Probably the more exacting public position was the office of deputy lieutenant that involved the raising of men, money, and equipment for the county militia.[50] William Brockman represented his county in both county and national positions. He was a Justice of the Peace and Deputy-Lieutenant for County Kent from 1689 to 1690 and a Member of Parliament for Hythe for the period 1690–1695.[51] The gentry, although a small portion of the population, provided a large part of the public government of their counties. The position as gentry brought duty as well as privilege.

Economically, Kent's "proximity to London encouraged specialization in wheat production in north-east Kent."[52] In fact, location helped the grain production in Kent expand 4.75 times from 1587 to 1638. Although agriculture was important to the economy, there was also an expansion of industry. Glass making was introduced in the area in the 1590s, and there was a growing market for a wide variety of manufactured goods.[53]

Terms for Women

Various terms reflect the tenuous positions of women during their adult life cycle. *Mother*, *mistress*, *goodwife*, and *widow* were all terms that identified women in relation to other women, to men, to their children, and to other groups. *Mother* usually referred to the female parent, but it could also refer to an elderly woman of a lower social class or it could refer to a stout or untidy old woman.[54] *Mistress* could refer to a prostitute, a woman hired by the parish to work for low wages, or a woman who "had control over servants, households and families, or men's hearts."[55] These terms not only fluctuated with age, but they also fluctuated with cultural considerations, social class, and economics. As with the term mistress that vacillates between a "lady of a manor house" to a "lady of the night," the terms for a woman can label them within the vast continuum of social respectability. Only one term, dependent primarily on visual signs of aging, remains constant: *old*. Affected by lifestyle, diet, work, disease, childbirth, and inherited genes, the physical signs of aging could appear at different ages. Generally, women were considered old at about fifty-two whereas men were not thought so until sixty-one.[56] As a woman began to stoop, so too, did the perception of her age.

The terms used to refer to women framed old age in three ways. Chronological old age begins when a set age is reached. In 1695, Gregory King identified those over sixty as old, and he calculated that about 10 percent of the total population was sixty and over.[57] Functional old age is reached when an individual can no longer care for his/herself. Lynn Botelho says cultural old age "combines aspects of these elements (calendar years and functionality) plus other variables, and determines the understanding of old age according to the community's particular value system."[58] Usually a woman was termed old after menopause, when the physical side-effects of plummeting estrogen levels and lower levels of calcium affected her looks. Changes in the physical appearance of the face and body of women—puffiness, lines, and bent posture—combined to make a woman look old before a man. Of course, diet, health, genetics, physical activity, and social circumstances influenced the pace of physical changes of the individual.

The Many Faces of Old Age

17th Century Nun's Prayer

> Lord, Thou knowest better than I know myself, that I am growing older and will someday be old. Keep me from the fatal habit of thinking I must say something on every subject and on every occasion. Release me from craving to straighten out everybody's affairs. Make me thoughtful but not moody; helpful but not bossy. With my vast store of wisdom, it seems a pity not to use it all, but Thou knowest Lord that I want a few friends at the end.

> Keep my mind free from the recital of endless details; give me wings to get to the point. Seal my lips on my aches and pains. They are increasing, and love of rehearsing them is becoming sweeter as the years go by. I dare not ask for grace enough to enjoy the tales of others' pains, but help me to endure them with patience.
>
> I dare not ask for improved memory, but for a growing humility and a lessening cocksureness when my memory seems to clash with the memories of others. Teach me the glorious lesson that occasionally I may be mistaken. Keep me reasonably sweet; I do not want to be a Saint—some of them are so hard to live with—but a sour old person is one of the crowning works of the devil. Give me the ability to see good things in unexpected places, and talents in unexpected people. And, give me, O Lord, the grace to tell them so Amen. (Source Unknown)

Although the source of this poem is unknown, its topic is not. Old women have been and are a topic of humor, hate, and horror. Written in the seventeenth century, the Nun's Prayer supports a caricature of older women as loquacious and overbearing. As the nun ages, she asks for "humility and a lessening cocksureness" and to be "helpful but not bossy." Agency and voice are the primary themes of this poem, but these attributes were not admired in women. In the supplicant position of prayer, the nun asks God to "seal my lips;" indeed, the society of seventeenth-century England desired the same for all women. Through an assortment of prayers, advice, and laws, women in general and older women in particular were asked to seal their lips as well. Publication was not the only public voicing denied to women, and a good reputation was not the only thing lost when a woman spoke out. As women aged, they often became the brunt of jokes—jokes that portrayed them as witches, sometimes humorously, but sometimes maliciously.

The image of old age can be seen in popular print culture: the penny chapbook, small pamphlet, and broadside. These books addressed traditional issues of courtship, marriage, and gender roles. Much of the printed pictures were used as decoration on walls and inside trunks, and they could be found where the mass population would see them on a daily basis—alehouses. "The very ubiquity of cheap print and its images of the elderly viewed, both at home and in public, strongly suggest that they were seen and known by all members of society, but especially among the lowest orders, toward whom they were directed."[59] The images presented in cheap print most often portrayed older women as physically ugly, never wise, and purely evil—primarily witchlike.[60] The humped back, toothless grin, beards, and walking cane of old age were a direct response to the lack of calcium in the diet, extreme physical labor throughout life, and decreasing hormones. All of these physical attributes indicated both old age and menopause. "In accordance with humoral theory, the nonmenstruating old woman, by virtue of her stopped menses, had become more male, as her body became hotter, and generally much harder."[61] Often, with the body changes, came a change of attitude—becoming more masculine with their sense of authority and wisdom. The maleness of their bodies and actions became a threat to patriarchal society. Additionally, the postmenopausal woman was a danger, since menstrual blood no longer flowed. Menstrual blood was generally considered "bad blood" that needed to be discharged from the body on a regular basis for good health, and which, if it was not expelled, collected in the body and poisoned the woman. This poison manifested itself in a very negative attitude and became the stereotypical old women as loquacious, argumentative, and overbearing.[62] Moreover, the end of a woman's reproductive cycle violated the moral and social codes that saw women within the role of a mother. No longer able to bear children and more liberated physically and psychologically, older women no longer fit into the ideal of femininity.

Although men were also affected by diet and labor, they did not show the telltale physical characteristics of age until about ten years after women. Moreover, their portrayal never diminished men as they aged. They still had status, authority, wealth, and the ability to procreate. Even in old age, men kept many of their roles of their youth. Even as poor men aged, they were often given less physical jobs to lessen the stress on their bodies. As young men, they had proved their ability to work; now as they aged, there was a nominal respect given to them that women were not allotted.

On an average, women who survive childbearing outlive men, therefore in most societies, there are more elderly women than men. The knowledge culled from their experiences has sometimes been valued and sometimes demeaned. Fluctuating attitudes toward age, in general, and aged women, in particular, in a society bring questions of gender into the forefront. Societies that value women merely as vessels to carry the species do not value older women. Communities that see women as an integral part of the whole value them in old age as well. To understand women in any society, one must understand that society's attitude toward old women. To understand mother's advice books of seventeenth-century England, and Anne Brockman's

Age Rectified, one must understand the position and perception of older women. Brockman asks women to plan for old age, and the possible effects of aging, because they are more likely to survive their husbands, and their position in society without a husband was tenuous.

Health, economic position, social class, and support, both familial and communal, affect how women thought about themselves as they aged. Aches, pains, ailments, and loss of hearing or sight all affected how old a woman considered herself. Sofonisba Anguissola (1532–1625), an Italian portrait painter who became the court painter for the Spanish royal family, painted into her eighties.[63] In addition to self-portraits throughout her youth, Anguissola has left the earliest known female self-portrait in old age. Art historian Frances Borzello describes Anguissola's self-portrait at nearly eighty: "she is still upright, proud, and strong."[64] At eighty, Anguissola still paints, still paints well, and still believes herself a good subject. Sara Mendelson and Patricia Crawford explain: "whatever a woman's social level, if she enjoyed good health she was more likely to be independent of others and to take pleasure in life."[65] Even approaching eighty, with wrinkled skin, Anguissola acts like a young woman—she paints the woman she sees in the mirror. By the age of ninety, Anguissola was no longer painting, and that seems to be reflected in her physical body. The last portrait of her is not a self-portrait, but rather a sketch by one of her admirers, Van Dyck. Borzello continues,

> Ten years later she showed herself as a frail old woman, with the flesh fallen from her face and the slight stoop that had finally bent her body. This same ancient face was sketched years later in 1624 by Van Dyck when he recorded his visit to her in a letter to a friend. He reported that her greatest sorrow was that failing sight had stopped her painting.[66]

Ten years later, Anguissola is a very different woman. Nearly ninety, her body and spirit register the ravages of time. Unable to paint and create on canvas, Anguissola, in the portrait and in life, begins to recede into the background. In fact, this is not the first old woman in the background for Anguissola. In 1545, Anguissola did her first self-portrait. Borzello explains, "the artist was about thirteen at the time, which is probably why she presents this unusual smiling self-image" in the foreground with an old woman in the background—her mother, a family retainer, no one knows.[67] The older woman adds a note of propriety while accentuating the artist's youth. Like many elderly women, the woman in the background is not linked with any man, and like many elderly women, she recedes into the background, unknown to posterity.

An elderly woman's economic position, as well as her health, affected her attitude toward old age. For those women who were financially secure, old age did not present extreme difficulties. For women who had always been poor, old age meant continued labor even with physical problems. Even those women who did not have to work for sustenance, often continued to work in the home. As men's physical and mental strength decreased, they could leave their jobs or be relieved of the more physically demanding tasks, but women continued to care for the home—and they usually did so alone. Unfortunately, women who were destitute had to rely on begging, parish relief, or various institutions. After the Protestant Revolution, parish charities had less support for the poor. The good deeds and charity required of Catholics were replaced by grace and belief in God, so donations for the poor dropped. Some London companies, such as the London Company of Fishmongers, provided assistance for the elderly widows of company members, but this was one of the few. Mendelson and Crawford explain that "this included immediate relief, pension and places in their almshouse. Usually the company increased pensions as the recipients grew older."[68] Although some London companies provided these funds, most rural areas did not have this advantage. For those women without some support system, old age spelled hardship.

Parishes did not want to accept the responsibility of caring for the elderly even in times of hardship, so they tried to force relatives to care for the old. Although many portray seventeenth-century England as a pastoral paradise when multi-generational homes flourished. The household reality actually consisted of the nuclear family—parents and children. In the general population, children who grew to adulthood worked and saved to get a place of their own to start a family. This independence often resulted in children living far from their parents, and often, far from responsibility toward their parents. Thomas Becon in "Of Duty of Children towards their Parents" expressed familial responsibility as follows:

> if their parents be aged and fallen into poverty, so that they are not able to live of themselves, nor to get their living by their own industry and labor, then ought the children, if they will truly honor their parents, to labor for them, to see into their necessity, to provide necessaries for them . . . forasmuch as their parents cared and provided for themselves.[69]

Poverty, childlessness, no living children, and parents living far away from their children sometimes worked against family intervention. In one study, 5 percent of elderly men were residentially isolated compared with 16 percent of elderly women, and one-third of elderly women had no relative living in their households.[70] Parents were warned not to hand over too much to their children, because children could become dependent on their charity. William Whateley told how "many a child puts his mother to after-throes more terrible, than those with which she brought him into the world at first. Many a father is in travail of his old child that knew not the labor of his first bringing forth."[71] To cite a similar analogy, King Lear, too, gave away his property to his two daughters, assured of their love. Once the property and power were theirs, their father became an intolerable old man. Lear had a third daughter, and Cordelia tries to protect her father from her greedy sisters, but dies in the attempt. The tragedy, of course, arose from Lear signing over his property before his death, thus, losing his authority. Anne Brockman advises women to rear their children with kindness, but she also warns about giving children too much money when they are young, since they will not learn the value of money. Additionally, giving too much money to a child only makes them want more, and then they wait for their parents' deaths. Brockman, cognizant of the power of money to either ingratiate or insulate, also suggests that mothers living with an adult child should keep silent about financial matters unless there are difficulties.

Family and Community

Much of the earlier research concerning the connection between parent and child in seventeenth-century England is rather bleak. Stone's seminal work on marriage and family in early modern England remains important in the field. He assumed that the link between child and parent was not strong because of high child mortality rates. Citing the loss of a large percentage of children before the age of six, Stone hypothesizes that parents distanced themselves from their children as a defense against their pain. Philipe Ariès asserts that there was no developed concept of the child until well into the seventeenth century—children before that were regarded as little more than miniature adults.[72] This negative view of the parent/child relationship has been hotly debated in academia. More recent research concerning early modern family life envisions a more loving, caring, and more "modern" family life.[73] Wrightson discounts emotional coolness toward small children, as well as parental use of psychological repression to break the will of the child. Although corporal punishment was commonplace in grammar schools, moralists advised using the rod at home as a last resort.[74] Anne Brockman also advises not treating children too severely. Indeed, she emphasizes parental duty as an obligation to rear children as degrees of rational beings—as they mature, children should be treated more like adults than children. John Locke also supported this attitude toward children:

> parents looked after their children because God had placed in them suitable inclinations of tenderness and concern, woven into the principles of human nature such a tenderness for their offspring that there is little fear that parents should use their power with too much rigor; the excess is seldom on the severe side, the strong bias of nature drawing the other way.[75]

Children must be socialized, and this process often entails some form of discipline, but it need not be harsh. Elizabeth Clinton includes parenting as one of the "works of nature"—the desire to do the best for your children. Locke, Clinton, and Brockman agree that it is natural to treat children with kindness. Brockman warns against severity, which can divide child and parent, not only in the child's youth, but in adulthood as well. Recent evidence, including those from Brockman and Clinton, suggests a much more gentle and connected upbringing during the period than Stone theorized.

This connection, though, did not create multi-generational households. The family portrait of three generation households did not exist in England on a large scale. When children reached their early twenties, they looked for forms of permanent settlement outside their parents' home. This independence often came about through marriage. Once married and away from their parents' home, children rarely expected to contribute to the maintenance of their parents in old age. Wiesner adds,

> Evidence from England indicates that middle class children were more likely to assist their elderly parents by providing them with servants so that they could stay in their own households rather than taking them in; the elderly lived with their married children only among the poor. Though we often romanticize earlier periods as a time when the elderly were cherished for their wisdom and experience, this was not necessarily so.[76]

Recent evidence disproves the assumption that extended family households played a large part in early modern England. The ties within the nuclear family may have been far stronger than previously imagined, but the ties across extended families seem to have been weaker than previously thought. Peter Laslett estimates that only one household in sixteen had a "generational depth of more than two in traditional England."[77] Most early modern English households embraced the classic American family unit—father, mother, and children.

Although generations did not share households, they often relied on each other for medical support, especially in the rural areas. Thus, the community of multi-generational inhabitants became the health center of the rural areas. Since elderly women had the leisure and experience, old age was also a time for nursing the sick. Their knowledge and talents were priceless in their household, especially in rural areas where they had to be self-sufficient. In rural Kent (30–35 people per mile), home of the Brockman estate, women who understood herbs and tonics were valued. As seen in *Age Rectified*, a woman with an understanding of medicine was a valuable resource for the family and community. Brockman advises women, that "if we have had opportunity to attain any competent Skill in Pysick, or Surgery, this will be a useful Charity, that will gain us Esteem for the whole Neighbourhood."[78] In addition to teaching daughters and daughters-in-law about medicine, elderly women attended deathbeds, childbirths, sick neighbors, family members, and friends.

Caricatures of Older Women

Authority, for some women, may have increased in old age. Depending on their health, social status, wealth, character, and knowledge, they could be seen as a valuable asset. The family was increasingly patriarchal in seventeenth-century England, causing women's roles within the family to shrink.[79] As survivors, older women were deferred to and respected, a source of advice for their daughters and daughters-in-law. Interestingly, Anne Brockman warns that reverence for the aged could become problematic if the elderly themselves were not open to suggestions. She worries that an elderly woman would become obnoxious, and thus, unbearable: "Old People are very apt to conceit themselves slighted without cause; and by talking much of it, they often put young ones in mind to do it."[80] Brockman warns that worrying and talking about imagined slights from younger people can actually encourage them to avoid their elders. For Brockman, judicious silence is the course of wisdom. Anne Llewellyn Barstow points out that "Older women were frequently notorious as scolds; those no longer beholden to father, husband, or children felt freer to express themselves and often said just what they thought."[81] One line of the Nun's Prayer expresses this sentiment when she prays: "Keep me from the fatal habit of thinking I must say something on every subject and on every occasion." The wealth of knowledge accumulated throughout their lifetimes gave women a basis for authority, whether it was welcomed or not.

The caricatures of older women also include the sex-starved widow who tries to attract much younger men. In a society where older men often married much younger women, this fear seems almost laughable. In fact, literature and drama relied on the humor concerning the sexual desire of an old man for a young woman.[82] The humor was not about an old man winning a young woman, but rather keeping her.[83] It was acceptable for a younger woman to want and marry an older man, but the reverse was not true. The Wife of Bath a character from Chaucer's *Canterbury Tales* is one of the earliest representations of widows on the prowl in England. *The Canterbury Tales*, popular since its publication, portrays the Wife of Bath as an often married woman who uses the Canterbury Pilgrimage as a way to find yet another husband. Her requirements for a husband include a well-endowed sexual organ and an even better endowed wallet. The story she tells, though, gives more background about the perceptions of older women. A knight rapes a maiden, and rather than sentencing him to death, the king allows the maiden and the queen to devise his punishment. The rapist travels the world for the answer to one question: what do women want? When the knight is at the end of his time, he meets an old woman who will tell him the answer if he grants her wish. At the trial, she whispers the answer in his ear: women want mastery over their husbands, love, everything—they want to be in charge. The jury agrees, and the knight is free. The old woman then tells him the price for the answer: marriage to the knight. He balks at the idea, but she reminds him of his promise and defines "honor"—keeping your word. The knight marries her, but will not have sex with her. The old woman, seen as ugly because of her age, presents him with a choice: I will be an old, ugly wife, but a good one, or I will be a young, beautiful wife who cheats on you with all your friends. After much thought, the knight tells the old woman to choose. She tells him his answer was the right one—she has mastery over him, and now she will be a young, beautiful, good wife. In the scenario of the young woman and old man, he can have her sexually, but he cannot keep her. In the scenario of the old woman and the young man, she can only have him sexually if she is young. Old women were never portrayed as desirable to young men.

In *The Duchess of Malfi* (1613) by John Webster, the widowed duchess is desirable. In fact, she marries her servant and remains in a monogamous relationship until murdered by her brothers. Her brother Ferdinand worries that the widowed duchess will have an affair with a "thick-thighed bargeman" and taint the family blood. Her other brother, the Cardinal, has an affair with a married woman, whom he murders to keep their affair a secret. Ferdinand does not see the actions of his older brother, the Cardinal, as deviate, but both brothers must stop their sister from sullying the family bloodline. They kill her, her husband, and their three children to keep the family line clean. Apparently, murdering women, children, and an innocent man do not taint the blood, as long as the sexually promiscuous widow is dead. In this instance, though, larger forces are at work and both brothers die violent deaths.

In William Congreve's *The Way of the World* (1700) an older woman, Lady Wishfort, who was wooed by a rake, Mirabell, seeks revenge. Unfortunately, she becomes the focus of a con by Mirabell; this time one of his servants is to marry her for her money. Although a rake has taken advantage of her, and will again, there is no sympathy for her. One of the younger women, Mrs. Fainall, laments: "Female frailty! We must all come to it, if we live to be old and feel the craving of a false appetite when the true is decayed."[84] Sexual appetite in an older woman is seen as aberrant, and this frailty warrants abuse by everyone. The play includes a dressing room scene in which Lady Wishfort applies too much make-up in an attempt to cover her age, and then, drinking too much alcohol covers her failure to do so. On some level, she knows she cannot succeed, and this makes the denouement of the play even more malicious—she is "unsexed," hence she must promise never to marry. Additionally, she must give an inheritance to her daughter and £6,000 to her husband, pardon Mirabell, and help her nephew get consent to marry the woman he loves. Lady Wishfort pays a high price for being old. At the end of this comedy, everyone has who and what they want but the old lady—she is left to wish for it.

Sex was not only the fodder of Restoration drama; it could also be found in an odd advice book entitled *A Bargain for Bachelors, Or: The Best Wife In the World for a Penny* written by Mrs. Susanna Fesserson, 1675. Offered "To young-men for directing their choice, and to Maids for their Imitation," the author begins,

> I am confident, Gallants! you no sooner hear this Tytle of, A bargain for Batchelors, cryed under your windows, but you'l presently conceit I am

> some old decayed Procuress that by chance have got a pretty handsome bit of temptation out of the Country, and that this is a Bill giving notice, where her Maiden head is to be sold by inch of Candle.[85]

Fesserson's bargain for bachelors is not the sale of rural maidenhead to the highest bidder, but advice on choosing an honest and virtuous wife. Fesserson first chastises young wits for dishonoring their mothers—by calling them whores—which reflects on their attitude about all women. They also despise and laugh at the name "wife." In so doing, they have distorted the true nature of an honest wife. Using her advice on how to choose a good wife, they would change their misogynistic attitude through marital bliss.

Fesserson pictures the attributes of a good wife's nature as those that relate to her husband. These natural attributes accept the husband as an inseparable second self, the guardian for his honor, "the perfection of a man," and "the elixir of temporal comforts"—in essence, the woman who serves and honors her husband is a good wife. According to Fesserman, a young man's mistress is to advise him, a middle-aged man's companion is to comfort him, and an old man's nurse is to cherish him. Although the authors of mother's advice books suggested subservience to one's husband, the degree assumed by Fesserson implies a type of slavery that sets itself apart from the other advice books. The author adds,

> She loves but one, and that is him she should, viz. Her husband, and she loves him because he is so, and if he prove cross or unkind it may exercise her patience, but never destroy her affection.[86]

In Fesserson's text, subservience to the husband assumes the force of absolutism. According to Fesserson, a wife loves her husband for what he is to her, not who he is as a person. Moreover, she never suggests correction of the husband's faults, only patience with them. This patience, of course, is all one sided. Fesserson tells men what to expect from their wives, but does not mention what is expected of husbands. This one-sided perspective reappears in the delineation of a good wife's choice; she "chuseth not a Husband by the strength of his back, nor at all considers the lusty Calf, or complexion."[87] The strong back and lusty calf, of course, belongs to a lusty youth, and the hope of sexual gratification should not sway a woman when choosing a husband, but the author never actually says how she does choose a husband.[88] By eliminating strength as a valid requirement, the argument supports older men as perfectly acceptable choices for a husband. The other advice books do not mention men's physical attributes, but focus on faith.

Although Fesserson cannot direct men to a good wife, she does itemize six rules for choosing a wife: look for piety and solid virtue, insist upon good breeding from honest parentage, do not accept a flighty woman, do not allow money or looks to sway you in your decision, look for the good proportion of virtues—just enough money for comfort, and

> the behavior to vanity or weakness. This is no laughing matter for Cowper. Though, Vertue, Riches, and good Nature are excellent things by themselves, yet joyned all together, they are not enough to Justifie your choice, unless she be fit to, I mean of a like humour, and agreeable temper to suit with yours.[89]

Apparently, men should choose the correct humor before the wedding, so they will not have to be patient with ill humor during marriage.

The extremely restrictive role models communicated to women and the egocentric prerogative presupposed for men in the text, as well as the confidence of the author, arouses suspicion concerning the gender of the writer. The excessive subordination of the woman evident in this text reflects a masculine desire for complete domination absent in the other texts. This stalwart perspective seems incongruent with the other seventeenth-century mother's advice texts and women's writing. I believe the author was a man.

Although the image of an old woman, powdered and primped for an assault on a man is a comic one, the stereotype permeated the society. In her diary, Lady Sarah Cowper writes,

> I met with Lady W——o, of whom it may be said she hath rent her face with painting. She is at least old as I am and hugely infirm yet affects the follys and aires of youth, displays her breasts and ears adorne both with sparkling gems while her eies look dead, skin rivell'd, cheeks sunk, shaking head, trembling hands, and all things bid shut up shop and leave to traffick with such vanitites or affection of superfluities which signifys nothing but weakness.[90]

Obviously, this was not written for comic relief or entertainment of others. Indeed, this perspective of older women was found in a personal journal, thus, expressing a private acceptance of the sexually starved older woman, who uses artifice to cover the ravages of time. Cowper's vitriol description of the woman illustrates disapproval and abject abhorrence, relating the desire to attract the opposite sex to folly and vanity. She had the financial and educational background to see the caricatures of the sex starved woman, and she found them pathetic. Cowper knew that no matter how much makeup Lady W. wore, how much breast she showed, or how many gems she displayed, her body was still old and undesirable.

Besides being considered sexually unattractive, older women were also portrayed as too talkative. Women of England lacked the agency given to men. Women, especially as they aged, became the butt of jokes and the promoters of fear. Elderly women who talked too much could be placed in scold's caps, heavy metal masks with sharp tongue depressors that often cut or punctured the tongue, by their husbands. Fitted in these torture habits, they were then paraded into the market square for public view. This image carried with it a strong message for women: be silent. Interestingly, Anne Brockman's advice could save an older woman from being despised by the younger generation, not only in the home but in the community as well. By moving the locale of her advice from the home to the community, her suggestions would be helpful to all older women. She suggests helping out in times of illness, keeping criticism to yourself and not interfering in other's lives. Brockman's advice could make old age a time filled with activity and people.

The authors of mother's advice books used the role of mother to justify their public speaking and avoid criticism. Entering publishing through their roles as mothers gave birth to their voices. The advice is valuable, not only as advice, but as a model of subversion. Even in the twenty-first century, the caricature of older women as loquacious and overbearing exists in popular media. The continued popularity of the 17th century Nun's Prayer is evidence of the continued acceptance of the myth. A serendipitous event, seeing the poster of the prayer on the friend's office wall, led to a search of the Internet. There, you can buy posters, framed art and pocket cards, as well as printed decorative copies—and all are listed as "inspirational" to women. The message continues to be sent and sometimes received—women, especially older women, talk too much and should make an effort to be silent.

Mother's Advice Books of the Seventeenth Century

> Be not full of tongue, and of much babbling nor use many words, but as few as they may. . . . For there is nothing that doth so much commend, avance, set forth, adorn, deck, trim, and garnish a maid, as silence.[91]

Turmoil aptly describes life in seventeenth-century England. Great rifts in the religious, social, and political fabric of England changed many lives, especially the lives of men. Individual talents, augmented with education, became vehicles for success and change within the shifting society. Unfortunately, women's lives, although changed, did not include the prodigious freedoms of men. Shackled to old notions of womankind,[92] women were often seen as a reflection of man—his needs, his desires, and his expectations—rather than as individuals. Relegated to the domestic domain, women took care of the home and the family, seldom going beyond private spaces without a man. Men, on the other hand, dominated the public areas, and through publication, attempted to dominate the domestic realm as well. Writing for publication, a very public act, was one venue where women experienced less autonomy than their male counterparts, even regarding domestic themes. Signs of male dominance in publication include the many advice and conduct books men wrote for women, all concerning domestic duties and expected behavior of women.[93] Some of the books by men, for women, include Richard Allestree's *The Ladies Calling*, a guide to proper living; Thomas Dawson's *The Good Huswifes Jewell* (1587), a general recipe book; Thoman Tuke's *A Discourse Against Painting and Tincturing of Women* (1616), a treatise against cosmetics; and John Taylor's *The Needles Excellency* (1631), a book of needlework designs. Throughout their publications, men told women how to act and designated their social and ethical duties. This male-authored discourse strove to teach women to discipline themselves under the surveillance of the male eye.[94] The existence of these didactic texts by men demonstrates a desire to mold women according to an ideal—an ideal devised by a male society. Of course, the continued publication of these texts also demonstrates the failure of this discourse. Many of the texts written by men tried to convince women to adhere dutifully to the prescribed ideal. Apparently, the lessons had not been learned, since the lesson was taught again and again.

In her essay "Surprising Fame: Renaissance Gender Ideologies and Women's Lyric," Ann Rosalind Jones points out that "there is a difference between being the subject *of* discourse and being a subject *in* discourse."[95] That is, lyric poetry frequently takes as its topic a woman as the object of the (male) poet's desire; there, "woman" is the topic/subject of discourse. Only as writers themselves can women become subjects *in* discourse—authoritative voices in an ongoing conversation with in their society. Although Jones is concerned with poetry, her distinction between being a "subject of" and a "subject in" applies equally well to advice and conduct books. Until women began to publish their work, women's lives were constructed through male-authored texts. From the seventeenth century onward, women became a subject *in* discourse by publishing their own advice books—books by women, for women. Although these female authors broke the code of silence by entering public discourse, they often did so in socially acceptable "feminine" genres: religious and advice tracts designed to help women and children lead a good life. Moreover, these women used a feminine voice when they did write, a voice formed in the domestic sphere. Although women chose to write in acceptable genres with a feminine voice, their ideology, as Randall Martin points out, often remained within the patriarchy:

> In particular not all early modern women questioned the patriarchal ideology that restricted and oppressed them in varying degrees; many accepted it either in whole or part, some with evident satisfaction, and so to some readers these authors may appear self-defeating and even irritating in terms of what we now believe were necessary steps for women to take collectively towards achieving greater access to education, political enfranchisement, and social justice.[96]

Although much of the advice given by mothers in these books adheres to the dominant ideologies of the time, they also departed from it. The most important departure is entering publishing as women. Indeed, their advice books focus on women from a perspective where no man could claim "natural" knowledge—motherhood. By entering the public discourse through the role of mother, these women sidestepped male disapproval, avoiding potential attacks on their authority as women. Mother's advice books challenged societal expectations by rejecting the code of female silence and introduced women's voices into the larger discourse of society through publication of their own works.

Few English women wrote for publication until the 1640s when social changes brought about by the English Civil War and the Commonwealth government enabled women to publish in increasing numbers. Patricia Crawford cites two important reasons for this change. First, with husbands, fathers, and sons away fighting, women tended and defended their homes. Second, engaging in political controversy sharpened their argument skills and led to further publications.[97] Wives, left to maintain their homes, often petitioned for the release of their husbands or lands from the opposing groups, Whigs or Tories. Women became an integral part of the life, business, and politics of their estates and country. This great upheaval in government—a change from monarchy to commonwealth—was only one sign of the permutation of English society. Even before the Civil War, religious groups including Anglicans, Quakers, and Puritans, began to shift duties of understanding the faith from a priest to one of individual responsibility. Each individual became responsible for his or her understanding of God's word through reading the Bible. Altering the locus of religious interpretation from the priest to each member required a literate congregation. Since religious instruction for the household was a woman's job, she needed to read the Bible to fulfill this essential role. With such motivation and justification, women from all but the very poorest classes learned to read—although not necessarily to write. Perhaps ironically, women's responsibilities within the domestic realm seem to have provided conditions newly favorable to women's writing for publication. Indeed, the role of mother and nurturer of future religious generations became a vehicle into public discourse. The responsibility of guiding future generations through education, both religious and social, provided some women with the technical ability—reading and writing—and the confidence to publish.

During the seventeenth and early eighteenth centuries, reading was normally taught before writing, so more people learned to read than to write. Education began with reading, and students did not learn even such elementary writing as signing one's name until much later in their educational life. Many people who could read a book, could not write a letter, or for that matter, sign their names. In the mid-sixteenth century, an estimated 30 percent of men and 10 percent of women could sign their names; by around 1715, the proportions rose to 45 percent for men and 25 percent for women. While the literacy of the lower classes remained below 50 percent, gentry and peerage were almost universally literate by 1550. Literacy of lower social groups such as husbandmen (farmers) fluctuated between 10 and 20 percent and showed no increases through the seventeenth century. The continued literacy imbalance between classes, J.A. Sharpe explains, was intentional: "most commentators, indeed, were convinced that education was something which was dangerous to offer too much of to the poor."[98] Sharpe adds that "educating women was seen as being as superfluous, and only a little less dangerous, than educating the male poor."[99] The culture and society of the time did not expect, or want, most women or men of the lower class to write. Moreover, their social position did not afford them the opportunity to write. Even women who could write did not have to write, since men had legal dominion over the women in their lives and signed all legal documents for them. The lower classes owned no property, effectively eliminating the need to sign their names. This educational, legal, and societal philosophy created a significant population of readers, but a much smaller population of writers. The communal attitude toward reading in this time period, for people often read aloud as entertainment, also made reading more important for a larger portion of the population. Frances Teague explains,

> Reading set a woman apart in early modern culture yet allowed her to reach others by teaching children or sharing a text with friends and family. The reading process allowed her to act; the metaphor linked women and books, however, constructed women as passive objects.[100]

Women and men of the lower classes, perceived as passive objects, could read texts that taught them how to act within their roles and their society, but they could not alter or add to those lessons by writing. Women could teach their children and share the texts written by men. This less-educated population could read advice books, participate in reading them aloud within a group, and discuss them, but lacking the ability to write, they could not add to the discourse by publishing their opinions.

Although publishing in the twenty-first century spells "success" for a writer, on the whole, people of the seventeenth century did not aggrandize publishing. Since manuscript circulation was not only the norm but admired, publishing was not necessary to validate a writer. Philip Sidney, one of the most famous of the Renaissance poets, never published in his lifetime, but he was a well-known and well-respected poet.[101] Manuscripts circulated regularly, and many of them were poems. These manuscripts gained huge popularity and respect for the author. Manuscripts then, provided a form of public audience, albeit a small one. Learned ladies and gentlemen formed the major audience for manuscripts, and they produced and circulated them among themselves. Although men played the larger part, women, specifically learned women, also played a large part in manuscript production and circulation. Financial stability of the family played an enormous role in a woman's education, since the most significant factor in their education during this time period was the willingness of their families to provide tutors to support their private education. The majority of women who participated in the manuscript society came from more financially wealthy and philosophically humanistic families who would support their education, financially and philosophically.

Publishing, on the other hand, provided a wider audience than manuscripts, including more accessibility to other classes and other countries. Published works could be easily reprinted, and for those who could not afford the book, it provided a stable form to copy or borrow. As the seventeenth century ended, respectable writers such as Ben Jonson, the first to publish a volume of his own works, chose publishing as a way of stabilizing and protecting their work from forgery.[102] Throughout this time, though, publishing generally remained a masculine pursuit.

Many women, taught only to read, were precluded from publishing. Even those who learned to read and write were rarely taught Latin, the language of academic and scientific publications that comprised "serious" publications. Thus, writing concerning "serious" subjects such as philosophy, science, and politics was considered a masculine pursuit. Certainly, women who could write often did so, but usually without an eye to publication. Enough letters, household account books, chapbooks, and family recipe and household remedy books survived in family papers to suggest legions of scribbling women. This writing was not considered "serious," since the topic stayed within the domestic and personal area populated by women. These one-of-a-kind manuscripts did not survive the way printed texts that had multiple copies did, and many were not considered important enough to keep, even in family collections. Manuscripts, saved in some family papers, found their way to libraries through donations. Unfortunately, until recently, many scholars dismissed domestic genres and did not study them as literature. In the last thirty or forty years, more women have become scholars, and they have rescued many of these texts.

Other barriers to women's publication existed. Writing for a widespread—and unknown—audience must have seemed largely incompatible with the womanly virtue of modesty, and publication, seen traditionally as a masculine form of communication, broke the tradition of feminine silence, too.[103] The idealized "modesty" included and encouraged silence in the home, and silence in public. Patricia

Crawford explains further: "In writing for publication, women risked their reputations. In seventeenth-century England, modesty was strongly linked with sexual morality: an immodest woman was an unchaste one."[104] When a woman entered the public by publishing, their writing hand was connected to other body parts—a woman who was immodest enough to write often faced ridicule as an immodest woman in other ways—a loose woman. Women's lack of education coupled with the societal ideal of woman as modest and silent made writing for the public difficult, and when writing was permitted, it dictated "safe" topics for those women who did write. Thus, the topics for women writers were located in the domestic, and the only respectable positions from which women could write were mother, wife, and mistress of a household. Chastity and modesty remained intact when a woman spoke within the confines of her roles, and the role of mother, held in most esteem, was given by God to women alone.[105]

Steeped in pious advice, mother's advice books of the seventeenth century broke the code of silence forced upon women, but often preserved the feminine ideal. The books were not written to win freedom from restrictions of society, but rather to reinforce the platitude of the ideal woman. The five popular mother's advice books published before the English Civil War tended toward the didactic and the spiritual. All of these texts encouraged an ethical and pious life within the confines of patriarchy. Rather than expanding the view or the role of woman, these five books reaffirmed the ideals of modesty, chastity, and piety, while often apologizing for breaking the law of female silence. The popular middle-class authors included

- Elizabeth Grymeston, *Miscelanea, Meditations, Memoratiues* (1604),
- Dorothy Leigh, *The Mother's Blessing* (1616),
- Elizabeth Josceline, *The Mothers Legacie to her Unborn Child* (1622), and
- Elizabeth Richardson, *The Ladies Legacy* (1645).

All of the middle-class authors apologize for stepping out of traditional woman's roles to write advice books for their children. A similarly pious book by another middle-class woman, *The Legacy of a Dying Mother to Her Mourning Children, Being the Experiences of Mrs. Susanna Bell, Who Died March 13, 1672*, was published a year after Susanna Bell's death. Her text is an autobiography of her spiritual journey rather than an advice book,[106] but Bell's autobiography is relevant here because it includes an introduction designating her life as a model for good Christian women and children.

In addition to the middle-class authors, an aristocrat, the Countess of Lincoln, Elizabeth Clinton, wrote and published her advice book, *The Countesse of Lincolnes Nurserie* (1623). Unlike the middle-class authors, the countess does not apologize for publishing. Moreover, her audience, women from the aristocracy, gentry, and wealthy merchant class, are not children, but mothers. Breast-feeding, death in childbirth, and child mortality were topics of interest to all women, however, wealthy women had an option to hire a wet nurse, and they generally had more children than women of the lower classes.

Child mortality rates in England were higher in the seventeenth century than in the twentieth century, so numerous mothers, including Elizabeth Grymeston who was the author of the mother's advice book *Miscelanea, Meditations, Memoratiues* (1604), did not see many of their children live to adulthood. In 1662, John Graunt estimated that 36 percent of Londoners did not live beyond the age of six years.[107] Unfortunately, the child mortality rate was even higher in the Grymeston household; eight of her nine offspring died while still children. While gravely ill and fearing her own death, Grymeston was compelled to give her only surviving child motherly advice,

> My dearest sonne there is nothing so strong as the force of love; there is no love so forcible as the love of an affectionate mother to hir naturall childe: there is no mother can either more affectionately shew hir nature, or more naturally manifest hir affection, than in advising hir children out of hir owne experience, to eschue evill, and encline them to do that which is good.[108]

Staying within the bounds of tradition and prescribed roles, Grymeston is obliged by motherly love to counsel her son and designate actions for a good Christian life. Grymeston, though, takes her own advice, when she decides to write to her son: "Be mindfull of things past; Carefull of things present; Provident of things to come."[109] As Grymeston saw nearly all of her children die, she is careful to keep her only surviving son alive, both physically and spiritually, as she provides for his future without her physical presence by creating a textual presence. Normally, her advice would be verbal, but her fear of death in childbirth compelled her to write this advice. In her book, she describes herself as "resolved to breake the barren soile of my fruitlesse braine, to dictate something for thy direction; the rather for that as I am now a dead woman among the living . . . ."[110] Grymeston's fear of an early death was legitimate; she died shortly after completing the text.

Grymeston's private purpose for writing, the spiritual guidance of her son, becomes a prudent use of the public sphere—the spiritual guidance of others—when her advice book is published. Motherly love, considered the strongest form of love that exists, justifies the desire to publish her work and to speak beyond the grave. Grymeston's advice book was published posthumously, and the identity of the volume's editor is probably Grymeston's husband. Grymeston's biographical information comes from the introduction, but little else is known about her. In a dedicatory poem to Grymeston, Simone Grahame aggrandizes her in the role of mother and nearly reincarnates her as the perfect mother. The work of this deceased mother, he explains, gives her life again: "Thou sacred worke giv'st mortall life againe."[111] This poem, written posthumously, creates an indisputable ethos for Grymeston. Moreover, the male voice of the poem legitimizes her authority as a writer. In death, Grymeston is and always will be the perfect mother.

Grymeston's book, the most literary of the advice books, not only includes her own meditations, thoughts, and experiences, but also draws from an assortment of literary works by male writers. Drawing on the authority of patriarchy, she focuses her knowledge, gained through life experience and books, for the salvation of her only living son. Elaine Beilin explains that "by doing so, she explicitly unites two main themes in women's writing in the Renaissance: the desire to reach out for all knowledge, to escape intellectually from domestic, private constraints; and the search for an appropriately feminine persona, subject and form."[112] Grymeston goes beyond the traditional silent woman when she writes to her son. She posthumously ventures into the public sphere in the traditional role of the loving mother, prepared to save her son from damnation at any cost to her own reputation.

In her epistle to the main text of the book, Grymeston supports education for her son as a way of going beyond animal needs: "without learning man is but an immorrall beast." The education she suggests is not focused on the Bible and self-examination, but rather on an eclectic reading list:

> And the spiders webbe is neither the better because wouen out of his owne brest, nor the bees hony the worse, for that gathered out of many flowers; neither could I euer brooke [do credit] to set downe that haltingly in my broken stile, which I found better expressed by the grauer authour.

God send thee too, to be a wits Camelion,
That any authours colour can put on.[113]

Grymeston supports education as a means to go beyond one's own thought process. Just as a bee gathers nectar from an assortment of flowers, education provides the learner with an assortment of viewpoints and experiences to form the foundation of their personal thoughts. Grymeston's diversity goes beyond reading to a diversity of mind. She actually supports mutating one's mind to an author's intent when reading a book similar to how a chameleon alters body color according to its environment. The most interesting point in this quotation, though, concerns writing. Grymeston will not write when another author has expressed the thought better than she. Apparently, writing the advice book reflects the lack of a text that expresses her counsel better than she can herself. This lack of a well-written text, by a greater writer, as a guide for her son further legitimizes Grymeston's decision to write—she can do a better job than those who preceded her.

Many male writers of the seventeenth century regarded modesty, in mind and in dress, as well as chastity, an exclusively female endeavor; however, Grymeston advises her son to "Let your attire be such, as may satisfie a curoius eye; and yet beare witnesse of a sober mind. Arme your selfe with that modesstie, that may silence that ventemperate tongue, and controll that vnchaste eye, that shall aime at passion."[114] Grymeston makes modesty in dress, speech, and action an attribute of the male as well as the female. Moreover, she does not suggest wholesale silence from her son, but rather silence as a sign of a practical mind, one that controls itself in all instances. If this quotation was given in isolation from any background information, then it could surely be attributed as advice to a daughter. Found in chapter one, a short line concerning how to live your life, it is, however, directed to her son.

Of special note, the second edition of Grymeston's text includes chapter seventeen, entitled: "Of Willful Murder." Although Grymeston addresses murder traditionally—as a sin—she also includes nontraditional commentary on political authority, treason, and the qualities of judges. This unusual topic may be the reason it was excluded from the first edition. Discussing murder as a sin, one designated in the Ten Commandments, Grymeston explains that murder is never a secret, since the murdered call out to God for justice:

> And no marvel, for the very blood that issues out of the wounds of the murdered calls to heaven for vengeance, and the very soul that by the means is set at liberty, ceaseth not to cry and sound in the ears of God.[115]

The victims of murder continually call out to God for justice. On earth Grymeston believes, a magistrate must answer this call in God's name by bringing the sinner to justice, searching for the truth, and routing out false witnesses. Grymeston expresses her expectations for magistrates:

> having the rule of nature before his face, *quod tibi fieri nolis, alteri ne feceris* [do not do to another what you do not wish done to you], it will manifest unto him what an execrable thing it is to spill either the blood, fame, or fortune of the innocent, in which three consists the whole discourse of wilful murder.[116]

Grymeston invokes the golden rule as essential proof that nature considers willful murder a sin too but adds the destruction of fame and fortune, a character murder to the physical murder. Obviously, she considers the death of one's reputation as devastating as the death of the body. As a woman, the death of one's reputation was essentially the end of one's respectable life. This topic seems an odd choice within the context of the first edition, and in fact, it brings up more questions about the breadth of Grymeston's advice. If Grymeston's intended audience is her only son, she strays from this audience by including a discussion of those in public office. Even though she expects her enlarged audience—no longer advising only her son but also those holding judicial offices—to use man's laws to assist God's law, she never implies or assumes a profession for her son, even a legal one. Furthermore the first edition consists of prayers, religious meditations, snippets of literature, and parables, whereas chapter seventeen, included in the second edition, although steeped in religion, is quite different. Martin explains that:

> having proved to be a profitable commodity for her male editor(s) in 1604, Grymeston [her husband and assumed editor] could risk venturing into culturally dangerous waters.[117]

Although these additions suggest a more worldly view, they are all addressed through religion—the sins against man are also the sins against God. The second edition makes the prayer public and active—beyond private prayer—as Grymeston calls for action within the society and as part of the administration of that society. Grymeston's desire for her son and his family is not just praying for a good life, but acting within the larger society as well.

In her advice book, *The Mother's Blessing* (1616), Dorothy Leigh, a widow and mother, addresses her three sons, George, John, and

William. Unlike authors of the other mother's advice books, Leigh intended to publish. She dedicates the book to a powerful woman, the "high and excellent Princesse, the Lady Elizabeth her Grace." Leigh's popular book, published posthumously, included nineteen editions from 1616 to 1640. With all these editions, her audience must have been a large one. Estimating literacy by textual evidence, the ability to sign one's name, it has been estimated that 30 percent of men and 10 percent of women could read in the 1640s.[118] Because reading was taught separately from writing, this estimation has to be lower than the number of people who could actually read. Even if these percentages do not reflect the whole reading public, they do indicate a large pool of readers, and listeners, for the many editions of *The Mother's Blessing*. The inclusion of the dedication to Lady Elizabeth reveals a marketing ploy that signifies the breadth of Leigh's intended audience. Considering the dedication, this book is not only for her sons, but for a much larger audience. The dedication could draw Lady Elizabeth's attention, but more than that, the dedication gives a certain legitimacy to Leigh's text.

In *The Mother's Blessing*, Leigh concentrates on prayer, how to handle servants, and the education of children—normally topics for a good wife, but certainly of interest to a young man looking for a wife. To help her sons choose the right woman, she lists the attributes of a good wife as a blueprint for a happy marriage. Since Leigh will not be there corporally to guide her sons, her physical text will be there to advise them. The need for this essential guidance in her absence legitimizes her entry into publishing while invoking the acceptable, even admirable, roles of woman, mother, and wife.

In her letter to the reader at the beginning of *The Mother's Blessing*, Leigh excuses her entry into publishing as a continuation of her roles and duties. She manipulates the role of mother to circumvent potential criticism and tells the reader: "I could doe no lesse for them [her children], then euerie man will doe for his friend, which was to write them the right way, that I had truely obserued out of the written work of GOD."[119] By working within the domestic realm of motherhood and the broader realm of friendship, Leigh expands the personal and feminine to the public and masculine—if a man could write to guide his friend, then she can write to guide her sons. Leigh again supports her public voice by citing her legal bond to her husband's wishes here and in the afterlife: "I could not chuse but seeke (according as I was by duty bound) to fulfill his will in all things, desiring no greater comfort in the World, then to see you grown godlinesse, that so you might meet your Father in heaven, where I am sure hee is."[120] Here Leigh is eternally bound to God to help her sons lead a life that will allow their souls to ascend to heaven—and that is the comfort she receives from writing her advice.

Leigh expands her publication argument further by exploiting her wifely duties to her deceased husband. She entitles her first chapter: "The occasion of writing this Book, was the consideration of the care of Parents for their Children," stressing her duty as a parent. If her children question her choice to publish, even if it is not "according to the vsuall custome of women, exhort you by word and admonitions, rather then by writing, . . ." and "so vnusuall among us," then she assures them that "it was motherly affection that I bare vnto you all, which made me now (as it often hath done heretofore) forget my selfe in regard of you."[121] However novel, her action is really an extension of her duty as a mother. Left as the only parent of her three sons, she must fulfill the duties of both mother and father, even if it means going beyond her role as a woman. Indeed, Leigh goes beyond one generation of her family, and expands to future generations, providing a model for her sons. She describes her purpose in terms reminiscent of apostolic succession:

> I thought it fit to give you good example, and by writing to intreate you, that when it shall please God to give both vertue and grace with our learning, he having made you men, that you may write and speake the Word of God without offending any, that then you would remember to write a booke unto your children, of the right and true way to happinesse, which may remaine with them and theirs for ever.[122]

Leigh hopes to pass on a tradition of writing to her sons, requesting that they, too, write an advice book for their children—essentially evangelizing the Word of God. Leigh preaches, if you may, an apostolic succession of advice from her to her sons and then to their children. Her use of "children" does not specify a gender, but rather assumes that the unbroken line of the right and true will continue forever. Her vision of a writing empire, beginning with her and based on the Word of God, is not only a familial affair. By publishing her work, she expects others to read her book and heed her advice—much like the Bible spreads the Word.

Leigh begins to chart a new course—a new course for marriage with her sons as captains of the ship. Although Leigh's discussion of chastity upholds traditional ideas about woman, she turns from the traditional focus of female obedience in marriage to a reciprocal relationship. Leigh advises her sons: "First, you must seek a godly wife, that she may be a helpe to you in godlinesse."[123] It is not good for man to be alone, but it is even worse to be with an ungodly woman. She warns her sons with the story of Salomon as an example—a bad wife can lead to idolatry and a life of sin. Moreover, Leigh cautions her sons that once a man chooses a godly woman, he must be a good husband to her. If the marriage goes awry, the man is at fault: "If a man hath not witte enough to choose him one, whom hee can love to the end, yet me thinkes hee should have discretion to cover his owne folly."[124] Leigh tells her sons to choose wisely and once chosen to love until the end. If, however, he does not have the intelligence to choose wisely, then he must discreetly cover his folly. Should he lack these qualities, "hee is unfit to marry any woman."[125] Since the male chooses the female, Leigh places the responsibility of a loving marriage squarely on the man's shoulders. Leigh also gives her sons advice on how a husband should treat his wife:

> then hee would chuse a godly wife, and live lovingly and godlily with her, and not doe as some man, who taketh a woman to make her a companion and fellow, and after hee hath her, he make her a servant and drudge.[126]

Leigh's vision of marriage mirrors a Protestant or Humanist marriage tract especially as she extols marriage as a couple, joined through love and godliness, who actually like and respect each other. The male still holds the superior position, but it is a position that is augmented by the female to create a measure of equality within marriage. Invoking the standard of Christ's love for his Church, Leigh wants her sons to lead their households with love, forgiveness, and mercy and in partnership with their wives.

This egalitarian attitude within the context of marriage filters down to the marital progeny: "I am further also to entreate you, that all your Children may be taught to reade, beginning at foure yeers old or before, and let them learne till ten."[127] Leigh specifies "all your Children," because all must become servants of God and country, and to do so, all must be able to read the Bible and governmental directives. This ability to read is, above all, necessary for her one obsession, private prayer: "Pray often privately, faithfully, and zealously unto God."[128] The attitude toward literacy and prayer continues beyond the nuclear family to the servants. Leigh instructs her sons to include the servants not only in prayer, but also in the ability to read the Bible. "If they cannot [read], you shall at my request teach them, or cause them to be taught, till they can reade the tenne Commaundements."[129] Leigh wants to guarantee that her sons will be surrounded by godly people, from the family members to the servants. Through this community of good people, Leigh hopes to insulate her sons from future evil. In accordance with this godly life, Leigh devotes a large portion of her "little book" (216 pages, the longest of the mother's advice books) to private prayer—she uses this public venue to support private duty to God.

In further advice concerning child rearing, Leigh supports one axiom of the patriarchy: chastity as defining woman. In chapter nine, she suggests giving children good names—names from the Bible—to emulate, fortifying them for a life in Christ. Chaste women of the Bible, of course, provide the best models for a girl. Leigh uses this discussion of names as a transition to the subject of chastity. According to Leigh when a woman lacks the penultimate virtue of chastity, she lacks all virtue, and the unchaste woman becomes idle and vain. Leigh does, however, include men in this formula for sin: "the vaine words of the man, and the idle cares of the woman, beget unchaste thoughts ofentimes in the one, which may bring forth much wickednesse in them both."[130] Leigh never blames the man's vain words as the catalyst for sin, but she does warn women to be chaste, watchful, and wary in their company of men.

Although Leigh suggests many names from the Bible, she excludes Mary, until, of course, she explains the obvious: "there was no woman senselesse, as not to looke what a blessing God hath sent to vs women through that gracious Virgin."[131] Using the story of Adam and Eve, Leigh twists the dominant ideology of shame and sin visited upon all women because of Eve's transgression to a victory over sin because of Mary's miraculous child:

> The man might say, The woman beguiled me, and I did eate the poysoned fruit of disobedience, and I dye. But now man may say, if he say truly, The woman brought me a Saviour, and I feede of him by faith and life. Here is this great and wofull shame taken from women by God, working in a woman: man can claime no part in it: the shame is taken from us, and from posterity for ever: . . .[132]

Mary giving birth to Christ transforms the shame of original sin by Eve to God's blessing of all women. In this instance, good deeds can wash away sins, even for a whole gender. Leigh interprets Christ's birth through Mary as an act of forgiveness by God through Mary, thus, emphasizing the female as deserving of God's mercy. Leigh then uses Mary to sanctify chastity:

> *Mary* was filled with the holy Ghost, and with all goodnesse, and yet is called the blessed Virgin: as if our God should (as he doth indeed) in briefe comprehend all other vertues under this one vertue of chastity.[133]

Leigh's support of women's ability to bring "man" salvation does so by supporting chastity as woman's sacred weapon against evil on earth, and the lack of that virtue, the basis for all sins.

Earlier in the text, Leigh seems to place the responsibility of chastity equally on the male and female, but then she suddenly contradicts this position and realigns herself with the patriarchy: "it is not enough for a woman to be chaste, but even so to behave her selfe, that no man may thinke or deeme her to be unchaste."[134] Chastity for women is not only a state of being, but also a posture of appearance—it is not enough for a woman to be chaste; she must also appear chaste at all times. According to The Lawes Resolutions of Womens Rights or, The Lawes Provisions for Women (1632) a married woman who is raped is dependent upon the support of her husband: "If a Feme covert be ravished, shee cannot have an Appeale without her husband." "But if a Feme covert be ravished and consent to the ravisher, the husband alone may have an Appeal."[135] In a society that perceives women as possessions, rather than people with rights, Leigh's attitude is unusual. She places chastity on both parties equally.

Leigh expands on women's responsibility when she discusses heathen women who will give up their lives rather than be defiled and uses these examples to imply women's innate need for chastity and, further, the acceptance of guilt. Modest and chaste maids who have been ravished "have either made away [with] themselves, or at least have separated themselves from company, not thinking themselves worthy of any society, after they have once bin deflowered, though against their wils."[136] Although ravaged against their will, unchaste women know their place: outside patriarchal society. Leigh never mentions the male ravisher, his sins, or his place in society. Apparently, the earlier defense of women, based on Mary's actions absolving the sins of Eve, does not apply once chastity is lost, voluntarily or not. Since

Leigh hints neither at possible absolution for an unchaste woman nor the possible collusion of a man in this sin, she contradicts her assumption of mercy and forgiveness of sins. Moreover, the patriarchal society's stress of absolute chastity for women is endorsed by Leigh, even when it applies to the innocent victim of rape—there is no forgiveness or place in society for the unchaste woman.

Although Leigh relies on traditional roles to argue for her freedom to speak, write, and publish, she also subverts the ideal of woman by using cogent, albeit patriarchal, arguments. Her wisdom not only shines through the traditional facade, but it also illuminates the influence women have on the future. By breaking the conventional role of the private woman and producing a public forum, Leigh negotiates a public role for women in the future. This contradiction between her loyalty to the patriarchy and her dismantling of one of its principles is just one of many contradictions in Leigh's text.

Like Leigh, Elizabeth Joscelin wrote *The Mothers Legacie to her Unborn Child* (1622) for her child. During her pregnancy, Joscelin believed she would die in childbirth and needed to leave written advice for his/her guidance. Death in childbirth was feared by many women even though most survived. Roger Schofield's recent estimate of childbirth mortality rates of the seventeenth century suggests 9.3 mothers died per 1,000 births.[137] Although it did not occur as often as women feared, the threat of death in childbirth was real. For this reason, Joscelin wrote to her child in case she would not live to guide her offspring through life. Moreover, the posthumous publication of her text became an act of heroism—a mother's ultimate sacrifice for her child. The popularity of this heroism can be seen in the number of reprintings—eleven between 1622 and 1674—and a Dutch edition in 1699. Randall Martin notes the popularity of Joscelin's book: "Aside from Queen Elizabeth's writings, *The Mother's Legacy* was the most widely reproduced original work by a Renaissance Englishwoman."[138] The Virgin Queen and the dead mother occupy space in popular publication—one has never given life *to* a child, the other gave her life *for* a child.

Joscelin's text begins with "The Approbation," written by Thomas Goad, executor of her will. Goad initiates the argument for women in the public forum by explaining the restrictions of the common law doctrine of covertures. That is, married women had no independent legal status, but were legally "covered" by their husbands. Since her husband was still alive, the covertures law prohibited Joscelin, and all women of this time, from leaving any civil property to her children.

A woman's legacy is one of intangibles: "Whereas vertue and grace have power beyond all empeachment of sex or other debility, to enable and instruct the possessor to employ the same unquestionably for the inward inriching of others."[139] Thus, the virtue of this text allows Joscelin to bequeath her moral advice in a public forum. Indeed, Goad declares this text as all the more worthy because it proceeds from the "weaker sex." Joscelin's value as an author does not rely solely on the commendable substance of her text but joins with her grandfather's distinguished reputation,

> Doctor *Chaderton*, sometime Master of *Queens College in Cambridge*, and publique *Professor of Divinity* in that *Universitie*, afterward Lord *Bishop*, first to *Chester*, and thence of *Lincolne*: by and vnder whom shee was from her tender yeeres carefully nurtured, as in those accomplishments of knowledge in Languages, History, and some Arts, so principally in studies of piety.[140]

Goad then recounts her extensive and intellectually demanding education under the competent eye of her grandfather to justify Joscelin's ability to write. The inclusion of her eminent grandfather in the introduction establishes Joscelin's ethos or character as a worthy and learned woman. Omission of problematic facts about her life and family also help present Joscelin as a God-fearing, learned woman from a God-fearing family. Although Joscelin's mother, Joan Chaderton Brooke, lived apart from her husband, Sir Richard Brooke, after their only daughter's birth,[141] Goad never mentions the unusual arrangement. He includes only the six-year-old Joscelin's promise to her dying mother, "to shew all obedience and reverence to her Father (Sir *Richard Brooke*) and to her reverend Grandfather."[142] Goad also praises Joscelin's loving marriage to her husband and her "true and unspotted love toward her dearest" husband. Goad's introduction argues for the moral, virtuous, and educated daughter, granddaughter, wife, and mother as a credible author, regardless of her gender.

A letter from Joscelin to her husband precedes the main text and explains why she writes her advice. Soon after conception, she had an apprehension of danger—her death during childbirth. Although Joscelin did not want to die, let alone die in labor, she was prepared to accept God's will. Although positive she would die delivering her child, she did not believe her duty ended there. She believed there was a good commission she "might doe for my Childe more than only to bring it forth (though it should please God to take mee) when

I considered our frailty."[143] Believing she would not live to protect and teach her child, Joscelin, after much soul searching, wrote her advice in a book for the child, explaining,

> I knew not what to doe: I thought of writing, but then mine owne weaknes appeared so manifestly, that I was ashamed, durst not vndertake it. But when I could find no other means to expresse my motherly zeale, I encouraged my selfe with theas reasons, first that I wrote to a childe and though I were but a woman yet to a childes iudgement: what I vnderstood might serue for a foundation to better learning. Agayn I considered it was to my own not to the world and my loue to my own might excuse errore: and lastly but cheefly I comforted my self that my intent was good and that I was well assured god was the prosperer of good purposes: thus resolued I writ this ensuinge I to our little one to whom I could not finde a fitter hand to convey it then thine own: which mayst with authority see the performance of this little legacy of which my childe is the executor.[144]

When she could find no other way to bequeath her message, she writes to her child. Joscelin's reasons for writing are all self-sacrificing. First, even though just a woman, her understanding might serve as a foundation of better learning for her child. Second, any errors she might write would be overcome by her love for her child. Third, Josceline's intentions are godly, and God, the originator of good purposes, gave her comfort. For these three reasons, Joscelin finds the strength of conviction to complete the manuscript. Joscelin stays within tradition by pleading humility and modesty for herself even while participating in the immodest act of writing. Believing she will die allows her to break the traditional role of the silent woman and produce a private work in a masculine format, writing, that can be used as a model for her child. Perhaps unwittingly, Joscelin uses the seemingly antithetical roles—silent woman and woman writer—to dismantle the principle of silence as a feminine ideal. Writing, previously an activity reserved only for men, becomes the activity of a loving mother. Unfortunately, only the fear of her death allowed her to stay within the ideal while working outside it. She presents this coherent argument to validate her personal writing, and she wins not only approval of the private text, but also of the public one. Joscelin proves women can write and should write, but, as the details of her argument demonstrate, they should not publish. Joscelin's husband, however, published her text posthumously, and he included an introduction that argued the virtue of publishing the text—Joscelin's own argument was not enough to convince the public that a woman, even a mother, should publish.

Joscelin's letter to her husband includes advice for him as well as for their child. Generally, she advises her husband to be vigilant in his role as the supervisor of their child without allowing sentiment to cloud his judgment. When the child fails in his or her duty to God or the world, "let not thy indulgence winke at such folly, but severely correct it." More specific advice includes providing the child with a good nurse, one of "milde and honest dispositon" whose house is not an environment for learning "swears and scurrilous words." When the child does misbehave, she adds, let no one "pitty it with the losse of the mother."[145] The loss of a mother should not excuse a lack of discipline. Her second specific point of advice concerns education:

> keep it not from schoole, but let it learne betimes: if it be a son, I doubt not but thou wilt dedicate it to the Lord as his Minister, if he wil please of his mercy to giue him grace and capacity for that great work. If it be a daughter, I hope my mother *Brook* [Leigh's stepmother] (if thou desirest her) will take her among hers, and let them all learne one lesson.[146]

Joscelin supports the education of both genders, but the female curriculum includes good housewifery, writing, and good works; other learning a woman needs not, while the male should be prepared to become a leader in the church. Joscelin wants her husband to oversee the education of their son, but if it is a girl, she wants him to give her to her father and stepmother. She explains further that women can have scholarly training, but it is one that a woman does not need to fulfill her wifely and motherly duties. Joscelin stresses the domestic realm for a girl, but she also wants her daughter to use more than a mere needle; she wants her to learn to write. In a time when women learned reading much more often than writing, Joscelin is still requesting an extra measure of education for her daughter. Of her own education, she reflects,

> I desired not much of my owne, having seene that sometimes women have greater portions of learning, than wisdome, which is of no better use to them than a main saile to a flye boat, which runs it under water. But where learning and wisdome meet in a virtuously disposed woman, she is the fittest closet for all goodness.[147]

Although Joscelin takes women's lack of power for granted, she does not exclude them from power. The education of her daughter is important; after all, Joscelin's own education afforded her the ability and opportunity to write this advice book for her unborn child. Extensive education, education beyond reading and writing, though, is not necessarily helpful to a woman and may, in fact, drive her beyond her capacity. This may be something Joscelin learned by experience. Her roles as mother, wife, and mistress of the household do not require further education than the basics of domestic education, reading, and writing. She contents that only when wisdom and learning meet for moral good is a woman like "a well-balanced ship that may beare all her saile." Although Joscelin's extensive education prepared her to write advice to her unborn child, the wholesale education of women beyond the basics might give this knowledge to women who are not wise enough to use it for godly purposes. The image she evokes of freedom on a sea of learning and wisdom contradicts a long tradition, even with God at the bow of a female ship. A woman need not wait for her deathbed to exercise the learning she has acquired, but it should always be used for a virtuous activity.

Joscelin returns to the shore of patriarchal tradition, while chastising society, with her suggestion to her husband concerning humility, "labour by all means to teach her true humility, though I much desire it may be as humble if it bee a sone as a daughter, yet in a daughter I more feare that vice, Pride being now rather accounted a vertue in our sex worthy of praise, than a vice fit for reproofe."[148] Joscelin castigates those parents who tell their children pride is necessary. Rather than esteem pride—Joscelin believes—you should first esteem yourself, and others will then esteem you. She values esteem (having high regard for someone), rather than pride (being elated or satisfied with someone), implying that pride can be assumed without substance, whereas esteem must be won through a full knowledge of self or other. Clothes are a useful metaphor for pride. The false facade of expensive material only constructs a vain individual without a moral center. Joscelin allows no false facade of pride for herself. At the end of her letter to her husband, she claims she is short of learning and natural endowments and only writes for the good of her loving husband and beloved unborn child, even after her extensive education under the tutelage of her grandfather.

Joscelin's advice to her child relies primarily on the Ten Commandments. These laws, coupled with prayer, private and public, can guarantee a virtuous life, and after death, the Kingdom of Heaven. Like Leigh, Joscelin includes the servants in prayer. Unlike Leigh, she does not expect them to read, but rather to listen. Joscelin explicitly addresses a son only once, and this advice pertains to the ministry. At this time, she explains the ministry is held in contempt, a position fit for the poor and younger brothers of the wealthy, but she adds that it is a position highly regarded by God. She asks her son to be a humble and zealous minister, but only for God's service, not for promotion. The modesty, humility, and faithfulness of a son would be as important to her as that of a daughter, although location (public for the male and private for the female) would change according to the gender of the child.

Unlike Grymeston, Leigh, Joscelin and Richardson, Elizabeth Clinton, the Countess of Lincoln, does not apologize for publishing her advice book *The Countesse of Lincolnes Nurserie* (1623). Indeed, her social position imbues her text with an assumed public agency not evident in the other books. This book addresses mothers, especially mothers-to-be, urging them to breast-feed their own children. Because poor women were bound by economic necessity to breast-feed their children rather than sending them out to strangers, they would not be a part of Clinton's audience. Her discussion of breast-feeding implies a vastly different audience than the middle-class audience of the previous advice books; Clinton's audience is upper-class mothers. Wealthy women were pressured to produce many heirs, and people observed that lactation appeared to be a natural contraceptive. Also, women were advised not to have sexual intercourse while nursing—another natural contraceptive.[149] Additionally, many authors pointed to poor women who looked old before their time as examples of how nursing would ruin their physical attractiveness. Of course, the poor diet, physical labor, and hard life of the poor were not mentioned as the cause for premature aging. Told they must give birth to numerous children to insure an adult heir and warned that breast-feeding would make them old before their time (and undesirable to their husbands), many wealthy women did not breast-feed. Clinton's birthright, both of privilege and experience, imbues her with the confidence to argue against the opposition to breast-feeding and that confidence permeates her text from its opening pages.

Clinton's dedication to "LA" flaunts her confidence as a writer. Stressing that this is "the *first* [italics mine] worke of mine that ever came to Print,"[150] she assures "LA" that her persuasive abilities, "kinde perswasion," will convince mothers-to-be to perform their duty—breast-feeding. Clinton's confidence does not end there, she presumes her text will be such a success that additional editions will follow.

Even Clinton's praise of LA begins with Clinton's own agency:

> for my part *I thinke* [italics mine] it an honour unto you, to doe that which hath proved you to be full of care to please God, and of naturall affection, and to bee well stored with humility, and patience, all which are highly to be praised, to give praise to any person or thing deserving praise, *I dare doe it* [italics mine], & for this is lovely action of yours I can with much thankefulnesse praise God, for all his gracious guifts of grace and Nature, whereby he hath inabled you, to doe the same.[151]

Clinton actively judges LA's authority as a good model for women. Moreover, her proclamation dares, without question, to make such a judgment her right. Clinton sees honor in LA's actions, and she is sure it pleases God. Clinton judges natural affection, humility, and patience as praiseworthy; even further, she thanks God for the forethought to provide LA with the tools to produce praiseworthy actions—in essence judging God as a good provider. Even though Clinton's authority as a writer continues throughout her advice book, the text itself does contain a letter to the readers by a man, predictably, to reaffirm the female author's authority.

The letter, written by Thomas Lodge, declares Clinton "*the* Noblest *and* Fairest *hands in this land to set pen to paper*."[152] Lodge constructs Clinton's character with her personal virtues as the foundation, and then asserts her mission, mothers breast-feeding their own children, as a virtuous endeavor. According to Lodge, this text is a "must read" because of the notable author, the rare content, the good writing and the brevity of the text, all assets that cannot, or did not, apply to the other advice books. In addition, Lodge compliments Clinton's writing for smoothness of writing and fullness of execution.

In the text itself, Clinton outlines her strategy in two steps: "First shew, that every woman ought to nurse her owne childe, and secondly, I will endeavour to answere such objections, as are used to be cast out against this dutie to disgrace the same."[153] Both steps rely heavily on God and biblical references for support, but in addition, Clinton draws upon her character as constructed in the introduction. As a woman forced to employ wet nurses, she knows the dangers that such delegation poses to the children. She also knows that her duty now is to rectify her mistake and convince women to breast-feed their own children.

By God's authority, supported by Bible stories of Sarah, Hannah, and Mary, Clinton makes questioning the value of breast-feeding equal to an admission of ignorance. Breast-feeding, Clinton says, is the action of "a true mother, of an honest mother, of a just mother, of a syncere mother, of a mother worthy of love, of a mother deserving good report, of a vertuous mother, of a mother winning of praise"—the perfect mother.[154] Furthermore, proof of breast-feeding as naturally ordained and given by God can be found in works of judgment, works of nature, and works of provision. Where she uses "works of judgment," we might use "manifestation of judgment," and this includes dry breasts for those women who do not perform their duties as mothers. The works of nature are evident in women, who naturally desire to do the best for their children. The works of provision give women breasts that produce milk to feed their children. Hiring a wet nurse desecrates God's will. Besides shirking maternal duties, a woman who hires a wet nurse compounds the sin against God—she takes the wet nurse from her own child. Moreover, trusting children to strangers can be detrimental to their health. Of the eighteen wet nurses Clinton employed for her children, only two were thoroughly willing and careful. In sum, God provided women with breast milk as a part of their nature and only the judgment of God should take that provision away. Addressing her use of wet nurses, Clinton admits,

> I knowe & acknowledge that I should have done it [breast-feeding], and having not done it, it was not for want of will in my life, *but partly I was overruled by anothers authority, and partly deceived by somes ill counsell, & partly I had not so well considered of my duty in this motherly office.*[155]

Although she does not name the authority who overruled her, it was probably her husband. Merry Wiesner cites the advice to remain celibate during breast-feeding as one of the reasons wealthy husbands often made the decision to hire a wet nurse.[156] As the belief that sexual relations tainted breast milk was rejected in the beginning of the eighteenth century, fewer husbands hired wet nurses. No matter who made the decision to hire a wet nurse, Clinton realized her error in doing so, and she needed to make amends for her "undutifullnesse." First, she humbly repents her sins to God. Second, she shows double love to her children to make up for her negligence. Third, she endeavors to prevent many Christian mothers from sinning in the same way. In essence, her mother's advice book becomes part of her penance.

The last known mother's advice book published in the seventeenth century, Susanna Bell's *The Legacy of a Dying Mother to Her Mourning*

Children, 1673, differs markedly from the others. First, the introduction, written by Thomas Brooks, is more than twice as long as Bell's text. Second, the advice is couched in terms of Bell's life experiences, which include spiritual visions. Brooks' introduction draws the reader to the text by building the ethos of the author, neither as a compliment to the reader, nor as direct praise for Bell, but rather as a good Christian whose life can be a model for a praiseworthy life. Brooks asks "shall I hint at few things?" which prove Bell's praiseworthiness. His "hints" consists of twelve attitudes, including sincerity, humility, charity and mercy, avoidance of sin, justification of the Lord, molding one's life to the Lord's, imitation of the saints, constancy in the ways of God, high valuation of Jesus Christ, casting a mantle of love over infirmities, evangelizing, and striving for a comfortable passage out of this world, numbered and explained in twenty-six pages of text. Brooks assures the reader that this autobiography of sorts was taken at Bell's deathbed, implying a trustworthy narrative. He not only declares Bell above the praises and envies of men, he also declares her text above question. Telling his Christians readers not to speak evil "(if they could) of those who for the main have lived holily, and died graciously, as this deceased friend hath done,"[157] Brooks recommends this odd tale as a model, and the ethos he claims for Bell is based on her devotion to God during the many hardships of her life.

In the short text written by Bell, she discusses her life as a Christian with an imperfect heart as a life that must strive for faith. After hearing a sermon about walking before God with a perfect heart, Bell changes her "condition, and the Lord provided for [her] a good Husband, one that feared God."[158] Throughout Bell's text, the fear of God and the behavior it produces, results in good provisions from God. Conversely, disobedience incurs punishment. Oddly enough, Bell does not experience a merciful God, even though she mentions Christ. Her God is a vengeful God who controls her with punishments and rewards. When Bell tells her husband she will not go to New England, she loses her child; when she submits to her husband and travels to New England, they arrive safely. Her experience rewards the submissive wife and faithful follower. In New England, Bell, the "poor ignorant creature," lives a good Christian life and is protected by God. Her obedience to and faith in God saves her from fire, not once but twice. The first time fire strikes Bell's neighborhood, all but Bell's house are reduced to ashes (Bell claims that thousands of houses were burned). She explains, "yet his [God's] love, was then manifested to me in the preservation of my habitation, when many better than my self were burnt out."[159] The second deliverance from fire occurs during an earthquake. As she languishes on her deathbed during the earthquake, she thinks of Christ:

> there hapned a great Earthquake which did shake all in the house, and my son being by me, asked me what it was, I told him, our Neighbours were all amazed at it, and knew not but that the world might then be at an end, and did run up and down very much affrighted at it; but I sate still, and did think with my self what a Christ was worth to my poor soul at that time. And then God made these Scriptures sweet refreshings, supporting and quieting my soul.[160]

The earth shook, clearing the fog that covered Bell's understanding of the scriptures. The clarity quieted Bell's soul, but her knowledge of earthquakes quieted her action. Since Bell believed in Christ, she was neither amazed nor afraid, but was still. Her knowledge of the nature of God allowed Bell to submit gracefully to death. In the past, when Bell submitted to whatever happened, something good happened to her. Perhaps, submitting to death, rather than fighting against it, allowed Bell to enter heaven.

The autobiographical form of Bell's legacy to her children does not express specific directives. Rather, the format of Bell's book suggests the parables of Jesus Christ. In narrative, Bell expounds the love of and obedience to God throughout her deathbed autobiography as lessons to her children. She tells her story, but also, and more important to her, the story of a good Christian woman whose last self-sacrificing thought is not for herself, but for her children. Bell tells her story, not as penitent, but as a model.

Fearing they would not be there to guide their children, some seventeenth-century Englishwomen wrote advice books for their descendants. Ever cognizant of their roles as mothers, wives, and mistresses of their households, they step out of the traditional roles to prescribe actions that would allow their daughters and sons to navigate successfully the waters of society while steering them to the eternal isles of heaven. Taking the helm, if you will, they went beyond images of the silent woman to voice concern for the future, charting a course within society.

Although all the mother's advice books discussed here have been pious and didactic, only one offers less advice and more prayer—Elizabeth Richardson's *A Ladies Legacie to Her Daughter*. This work consists of three books of prayers advising modesty, humility, and faithfulness. Written during the years 1625–1638 and published in 1645, these volumes include prayers for all occasions, and then some: "A Prayer for the Ladies day, before we go to Church" (Book I), "The Prayer for Tuesday Morning" (Book II), and "A Sorrowfull Widows Prayer" (Book III), to name a few. Writing for her daughters and daughters-in-law, she defends her daring venture into publishing:

> I have adventured to bear all censures, and desire their patience and pardon, whose exquisite judgments may find many blameworthy faults, justly to condemn my boldness; which thus excuse, the matter is but devotions or prayers, which surely concerns and belongs to women as well as the best of men.[161]

Her faith dispels fears of breaking the code of silence as the legacy to her daughter, because prayer and devotion will help her lead a virtuous life. Richardson advises daily prayer, in the service and glory of God, as a way to a good life, and she uses the publication to serve God in the public arena.

The domestic sphere of marriage and motherhood dominated the lives of women, but the authors of mother's advice books entered the public sphere with the stated purpose of helping their children. Reaffirming the ideals of modesty, chastity, and piety, they also affirmed education and some semblance of equality and agency for women. Although none can be termed "feminist" by a twenty-first-century definition, they all dismantle the silent woman as an ideal. The continuum of change, the expanded view of women and their abilities, can be seen in these texts. As Virginia Woolf points out, "books continue each other, in spite of our habit of judging them separately."[162] As the authors of mother's advice have shown, a "good woman" is not just a godly woman; she is a woman who breaks the bounds of the private and enters the public forum for a cause—to be heard. The shifting within the continuum of changing views of women by women, their concerns and duties, is evident in a later mother's advice book, *Age Rectified*. While earlier advice books focus on piety, self-sacrifice, and chastity, *Age Rectified* reenvisions the duties of a mother. Brockman changes the role of mother as enforcer of Christian values to one of guide to ethical choices. In essence, her vision of mother lets the children go as they mature to hold on to them in adulthood. Rather than dictating actions, Brockman models actions and allows children to make their own decisions. Incorporating John Locke's philosophy of rational beings into child rearing, Brockman's strategies produce an independent adult with natural parental ties. Still seen within the context of wife, mother, and mistress of the household, the focus becomes strategies that can improve an aged mother's life. This new attitude refocuses a mother's lens, moving her from the background to the forefront. In this central position, she is still concerned with providing her children with lessons for a good life, but these lessons are also providing her with a retirement plan—a place in her adult child's household. Brockman's text continues other mother's advice books by looking to the future—she advises mothers to use the agency within their roles for their future benefit.

2

The Author and the Text

For over three hundred years, the only published textual evidence of Anne Glydd Brockman (1658–1730) has been the Glydd family crest placed in pretense (a small Glydd family crest superimposed on a larger Brockman family crest) on the Brockman coat of arms (figure 2.1). The family history, *Record of the Brockman and Drake-Brockman Family*, 1936,[1] contains little more than basic facts about her—the family tree diagrams her parentage, her marriage, and the birth of her children. The text includes figures of the changing family crest. Although the dates of Anne Glydd Brockman's death and her marriage to William Brockman are duly noted on the family tree, neither her birth date nor any other information about her is included.

Figure 2.1 The Brockman family crest in the late seventeenth century. David Henry Drake-Brockman, *Record of the Brockman and Drake-Brockman Family*. Lindfield, Sussex, England: D.H. Drake-Brockman, 1936, 101.

Born in 1658, Anne Glydd was the last child of Richard Glydd, Master of the Tallow-Chamber's Co., who, according to the Drake-Brockman family history, died in 1666. In her common book, Brockman's mother, Anne Glydd Sr., lists Richard Glydd's date of death as November 24, 1658, less than two months after Brockman's birth. Beginning in 1650, Glydd Sr. had eight children whose births were spaced approximately one year apart. This series of births ended with Brockman's birth, supporting the 1658 date as that of her father's death.

Brockman grew up without a father, and she only knew five of her seven siblings. Two died within weeks of their births, and two other siblings were dead by the time Brockman was four years old. Of the eight children, four lived to maturity, Elizabeth (the second—she was named after her sister who died at six weeks) died at twenty-four, John died at thirty-nine, Martha died at forty-two, and Anne (the second—she was named after her sister who died at seven weeks) died at seventy-two. Since she was still writing in her common book in 1697, Glydd Sr. survived all but one of her children, and she saw the birth and survival of all of her nine grandchildren until her own death (1718, suggested by Brockman's letter).

Although Brockman's brother John lived for thirty-nine years, there is no mention of his marriage or any offspring. When Glydd Sr. lists her son's death in her common book, she remarks that he died "before hee was usefull in his Genaration to man." This comment may refer to dying childless as his lack of usefulness in his generation. Although Martha Glydd Drake did not have her first child until the age of thirty, she did marry and have children before her death at forty-two. She probably married a year before the birth of her first child, which is close to the period's average marriage age for women—twenty-six. Brockman herself did not marry until the age of thirty-four, nine years older than the average marriage age in this time period. The mean age was calculated from a sample of twelve English parishes between 1600 and 1789, and it included all social classes of the parish.[2] Gentry and aristocracy normally married younger than the general population who had to get steady jobs and accumulate funds before marriage. Since wealthy families needed heirs for the estates, most of the gentry and aristocracy married, especially the males, to carry on the family name. The oddity of marriage-less male children begun with the John Glydd continued on to Brockman's sons as well, affecting the future of both the family estates and the family name.

Anne Brockman became coheiress, with her sister Martha Drake, to the Glydd family fortune. Her mother lived in the family home,

Pendhill, Surrey, Bletchingley County until her death.[3] Glydd Sr. lists the Brockman marriage date as December 22, 1692, only days before the change of the year. According to the Drake-Brockman family history, Anne Glydd Jr. married Sir William Brockman at Lambeth Chapel.[4] As gentry in the region of Kent, home of the Canterbury Cathedral, it is no surprise that Dr. John Tillotson, Archbishop of Canterbury performed the ceremony. Both William and Anne were in their mid-thirties, he thirty-five and she thirty-four—much older than the average age at marriage for the general population, the mid-twenties.[5] The couple settled in the Brockman family home, Beachborough, Kent for their married life. When Brockman married Sir William, she became Lady Brockman, an official member of the gentry, and at the age of thirty-five, Brockman began to have children.

Comprising 2 to 3 percent of the population, most of the gentry of Kent had been residents for 100 years.[6] This long history together formed a county with a record of close community ties, and that community, especially the gentry, tended to intermarry.[7] In 1640, 62 percent of gentry marriages were with other Kentish families.[8] The Glydd-Brockman marriage was slightly different, since Glydd came from the neighboring county of Surrey. As so often happened when daughters inherit, the Glydd family home in Surrey was sold after Glydd Sr.'s death, and the Brockmans, as well as the later Drake-Brockmans, stayed in Kent. Although the Glydd family estate was lost in this marriage, the family arms remained a prominent part of the Brockman family crest of arms.[9]

Throughout Anne and William's marriage, the Brockmans lived at the family manor, Beachborough.[10] There, they produced three sons, William, James, and John. Both William (1693–1721) and John (?–1739) died young, while James (1696–1767) lived to seventy-one. All of Anne Brockman's three sons branch off the family tree, but the Brockman branch ends there. None of her sons married, so James, at seventy-one, bequeathed his estates to his mother's great nephew, Ralph Drake, and his wife, Caroline Brockman, a cousin of his father's. Beachborough, like Pendhill, would change hands. This bequest, passed by an Act of Parliament, altered the family name from Brockman to Drake-Brockman, a constant reminder of Anne Glydd Brockman's influence on her adopted family by uniting a Glydd descendent (from her sister, Martha Glydd Drake) with the Brockman name. The last of the Brockmans, and many successive generations of the Drake-Brockmans, are buried at the family church, St. Nicolas, in Newington, Kent. All these facts can be found in the Brockman family history, but little else. Analysis of her textual remnants—her letters and *Age Rectified*—can provide a better notion of Lady Anne Brockman, wife, mother, and author.

Lady Anne Brockman was an able mistress, educated, financially stable, creative, and forthright. She could write well, and she had no qualms about expressing her opinions. The Brockman Papers in the British Library, London, contains three creative works in her hand: two poems and the handwritten treatise, "Age Rectified," listed as a copy of the printed text. Saved for nearly four hundred years, the marginal notes, signatures, and page breaks, as well as the corrections, spelling, and editing changes, now speak beyond the advice of the manuscript to name the author—Anne Glydd Brockman (see chapter 3 for the detailed argument).

More about Brockman, both Lady and author, can be gleaned from an analysis of her papers found in the Brockman papers—her four letters and her tract concerning aging, child rearing, and motherhood, *Age Rectified*. Generally restricted to the roles of wife, mother, and widow, many women writers wrote in these capacities, a form of self-representation in order to create an authoritative voice to address their audience. Roger D. Cherry states that

> decisions about self-portrayal are not independent, but vary according to the way in which writers characterize their audience and other facets of the rhetorical situation. A better understanding of self-representation in written texts can thus contribute to a more complete understanding of how writers construct rhetorical situations in the act of composing.[11]

Brockman, like other authors of her time, chose her audience, and using her knowledge of her readers and her own experiences, she wrote to capture the "ear" of her chosen readers. *Ethos* and *persona* are two relevant terms for discussions of self-depiction in written texts. Ethos, the self-representation of one's moral reliability, can be constructed by the author's use of a particular persona, a typified voice or self-characterization. Persona refers to a particular social role a writer assumes within her discourse community to access or connect with the reader. Persona is the constructed face of the author, and ethos is the reputation accorded to the author based on the persona. Both ethos and persona build credibility for a particular purpose. This process involves assessing the audience and constructing a discourse that gives the author integrity. After gauging the audience, the historical author builds upon her reputation or good character by assuming a persona or mask, which portrays the author in a certain role within the discourse community in which she is operating, enhancing the credibility of the author and the text. Brockman integrates her roles as mother, wife, and mistress of a large estate to achieve her ethos or credibility. She uses these personae, her assorted cultural positions, to cobble together a sense of authority, a credible, culturally forceful ethos.

In her letters, Anne Brockman reveals her roles as wife, mother, and mistress of a large household by discussing estate business, worrying about the health of family and friends, ministering to her family, and managing the large manor house. She discusses these same topics in her tract *Age Rectified*.[12] Brockman becomes the authority who gives advice on how to achieve a better life as women age and must rely on their adult children. At fifty-one, Brockman recommends procedures that can insure an old woman's place in the hearts and homes of the younger generation. Unlike most of the authors of popular seventeenth century mother's advice books, Brockman is not writing for her children, but for other mothers, more precisely, mothers of the upper classes. Moreover, she is not worried about dying in childbirth—an advantage of age and menopause. She is unapologetic for writing, and her advice is more secular than religious. Although Grymeston drew in many male authors when she wrote her advice book, Brockman employs only one. Drawing from *Some Thoughts Concerning Education* (1699) and *Two Treatises of Government* (1690),[13] Brockman weaves together Locke's thoughts about child rearing and education into her text. Unlike most of the other mother's advice book authors, Brockman does not need an introduction written by a man to validate her work. In fact, Brockman does not use her name to give substance to her tract, but rather, she relies on her persona based on feminine roles within the society. Brockman uses her real life roles and knowledge of those roles to build her persona within the text. Signing her text as one of the same sex, Brockman did not use her name to authenticate her advice book, but her persona as a woman.

In Brockman's introduction, she points out that advice is seldom given to the aged, who are either venerated or thought ridiculous. She also expresses her fear that the aged do not want to admit their faults and this lapse creates difficulties with the younger generation. Her intention for this manuscript is as follows:

> to persuade those concern'd That it is possible to acquire such a Disposition of Mind . . . As may preserve us in a good degree from

> being Obnoxious to others; when by keeping a Serene Temper we may continue in some measure still usefull to the Generation we live in.[14]

Brockman, although critical of the attitude of many older women, empathizes their position within the family and the society. She writes to persuade women like herself to create an ethic that will enable them to remain useful to and accepted by the younger generation. To build on this point, Brockman states that her own aging gives her the perspective to identify problems and formulate solutions. At fifty-one, Brockman had probably gone through or was experiencing menopause, a physical sign of aging for women. She explains: "my own declining Years puts me on these Thoughts, as knowing Temptations are best provided against when discern'd at some distance." Brockman is no longer just "of the same sex" as her reader; she is also invested in finding a solution to the generation gap as it concerns women. Her distance from old age—upper-class women were usually perceived as old at about sixty, at least another nine years away—allows her to observe the domestic unhappiness of many families that develops in the void between generations and to ascertain "it worth while to consider how much we have it in our powers to remidie these inconveniencies." Although Brockman never explicitly states that she is a mother, she identifies herself with the respective "neighborhoods" of mothers, and she uses the inclusive "we" throughout the discussion. Together with those concerned, "especially with regard to our particular Relations, as Mothers, wives, & Mistresses," the author will identify the problems facing older women and devise a solution.[15]

As a mother who writes for publication, Brockman reflects on the conduct of parents during child rearing. She addresses child rearing strategies from the perspective of cause and effect and asks whether the severity of hand that keep children from evil may have also keep them at a distance. She demonstrates a progressive attitude when she states, "severity can then be of little use" when rearing children.[16] Writing in the late seventeenth century, John Aubrey recalled that his parents "were as severe to their children as their schoolmasters." As a result, "the child perfectly loathed the sight of his parents as the slave his torturer."[17] Brockman warns that severity will not only breed contempt in your children, but it will also make them "shun & avoid our company & so put themselves out of the way of being reclaim'd by our friendly Advice, good Example, & handsome Insinuations, which might take some hold of them in proper seasons."[18] Although corporal punish may have been common in many homes and schools of the period, John Locke, like Brockman, spoke against violence as a teaching pedagogy:

> Before they go, they Principle them with Violence, Revenge, and Cruelty. *Give me a blow that I may beat him*, is a Lesson, which most Children every Day hear: And it is thought nothing, because their Hands have not Strength to do any Mischief. But I ask, Does not this corrupt their Minds?[19]

Both Brockman and Locke worry about violence corrupting the minds and attitudes of children toward their parents, creating a chasm between parent and child that may not be mended. Both question corporal punishment as a teaching strategy for it teaches nothing but fear.

Although Brockman is opposed to severe treatment of children, she does not exclude parents who have been too severe in the past from becoming good parents, with her advice, of course. Those who have been too severe with their young children can still save their relationship with them by showing the maturing child indulgence as they become adults. By finding a solution that will save those parents from being termed "bad," Brockman finds a solution that enables them to regain the love of their children. She advises a growing tolerance as the children approach adulthood: "to convince them that we did it only to bring them to the knowledg of themselves and to the obedience due a Superme Power."[20] By having parents explain their severity as a pedagogical strategy, rather than a desire to inflict pain, Brockman's advice clears the air, as you will, and shows the rational adult child respect by presenting them with a rational argument.

Brockman's discussion of child rearing takes a very twentieth-century twist when she discusses the parents and the time they allot for their children. Although the Brockman's were wealthy, they still had the responsibilities of the estate business, as well as Sir William's political positions.[21] When Sir William was away, Brockman ran the estate. Even though she was a stay-at-home mom, she was also a working one. The responsibilities of business and a social life can drain time from the family coffers, especially from the children. Brockman addresses this by focusing on the family as a business that needs as much attention for future success as any other:

> I know nothing that can excuse Parents from takeing some part in forming their [children's] minds at least in their tender years when some

> Happy impressions may be made; Then even their necessityes, who labour for Bread, may allow some leisure for this so necessary Work.
>
> But I doubt it is often such as have most leisure that least care to set bout this Business, thinking it will give interruption to their Company, and Diversions. How just then is it that in years they shou'd retaliate this Usage? This Reflection should move us to seek pleasure in conversing with our Children; and seeking we shall surely find it, by considering their improvements are owing to our Labour: and we shall so distinctly discern their Tempers, as to know how the better to dispose other Occurrences of Life.[22]

As the desire to succeed in business overshadows the family, young children are often neglected. Brockman reminds parents who neglect their small children that they may in turn, be neglected by their adult children. This circle of neglect can be broken by conversation with children during the crucial years of childhood. By building a foundation of parent/child interaction early in life, the parents are building an annuity of sorts. Banking upon the emotional connection from childhood, an emotional annuity, the parent can draw upon the account when old age necessitates support from their adult children.

Brockman creates a sense of authority and connection, both for the parent and the child, by relating the freedom of adults to the freedom of growing children: "Tis very hard for freeborn Rationals to live always under awfull checks & restraint." After years of fighting the power of an absolute monarchy, each Englishwoman reading this manuscript would be sympathetic to the ideal of free born rationals. Moreover, Brockman then compares the rearing of a child with managing a government: "Government is here only to be used of the Benifit of the governed; with watchfull discipline we are to train them up in that they shou'd goe."[23] Brockman was born two years before the restoration of the monarchy in England and probably knew that a major cause of the civil war was Charles I's insistence to rule as he saw fit without explaining himself to Parliament. The assumption of absolute monarchy by Charles can be seen as a macrocosm of the family when parents assume an absolute dominion over their children. Brockman's audience would be sympathetic to this view from the public standpoint of government as well as the personal standpoint of the family unit.

Brockman's comparison of the political government and the parental government draws from John Locke's *Two Treatises of Government* (1690). For Locke, children grow to become rational beings, and the power a parent has over a child changes with maturation:

> Their parents have a sort of rule and jurisdiction over them, when they come into the world, and for some time after; but it is but a temporary one. The bonds of this subjection are like the swaddling clothes they are wrapt up in, and support by, in the weakness of their infancy: age and reason as they grow up, loosen them, till at length they drop quite off, and leave a man at his own free disposal.[24]

Both Brockman and Locke understand that support of and rule over children is a necessity for their understanding and safety. Both see a difference between a child who must be guided to or confined by the right path and a rational adult who is free to choose his/her own path.

Responsibility for good parenting does not end with lessons for a good life. Rather than stressing prayer, Brockman stresses conversation with children as a way of becoming familiar with and guiding them. Locke, too, sees a familiar relationship as the best relationship with a son: "If you would have him stand in awe of you, imprint it *in his Infancy*, and, as he approaches more to a Man, submit him nearer to your Familiarity: So shall you have him your obedient Subject (as is fit) whilst he is a Child, and your affectionate Friend when he is a Man."[25] When favoritism rears its ugly head in a family, Brockman warns, "the Disquiet of the whole Family is almost inevitable, where one private Favorite is set up, to engross what others might equally claim."[26] Brockman sees the family as a unit held together by the roles of each member. When one is seen above the others within the same role, one child given preference above another, the fragile family unit is threatened, much like a parent's instance to rule an adult child threatens the family. Brockman considers roles important, but she realizes that roles shift, sometimes they are equal, as child to child, and sometimes they shift as with a maturing child to parent. As Brockman proceeds throughout this tract, it is the role within the family that supersedes the individual.

Brockman's plan for old age begins early in life with child rearing strategies. She reminds her readers that nature appoints the strong to care for the weak. As a child comes to adulthood and a parent enters old age, their roles reverse. Through the aging process, the child transforms from cared for to care giver. Brockman's retirement plan—her social security, if you will—begins with a solid foundation of respect between parent and child to become a solid support for the aging mother when the adult children become the stronger. Unlike the religious doctrine that charges children to venerate parents simply because they are parents, Brockman believes that

> it is the occasion of great Disappointments and Uneasiness, That Parents expect their Children shou'd pay them an Observance almost to Adoration when grown up, tho perhaps they owe little more to them than their Birth, and such a Provision as the Law inforceth: as if they were given only for our behoof, and not rather we appointed as Guardians to take care of them.[27]

Brockman explicitly states that parents are appointed guardians of their children, and children should not be required to pay their parents deference to the point of adoration. Her stance mirrors Locke's: "it is one thing to owe honor, respect, gratitude and assistance; another to require an absolute obedience and submission."[28] For Brockman and Locke, adulthood merits equality. Brockman warns that as the roles of weak and strong transpose, the quality of the transposition depends on the quality of the early relationship. The rationale of equality and liberty employed by Brockman supplants mere duty supported by the Christian ideals of the previous mother's advice books.

Brockman advocates accepting adult children as adults, and she especially stresses financial responsibility to insure domestic tranquility. By linking the adult child's responsibilities and freedoms with that of the parent, "If we are allow'd the freedom to chuse for our selves, it is enough; we may as freely let others do the like," she argues for a domestic strategy that avoids domestic unhappiness. Locke relates this to age as well as preference: "You must consider, that he is a Young Man, and has Pleasures and Fancies, which you are pass'd. You must not expect his Inclinations should be just yours, not that you at Twenty he should have the same Thoughts you have at Fifty."[29] Brockman emphasizes, "Let them spend no more than what's their own, and I would not much quarrel at the manner of it,"[30]—an advice that is especially important to a woman who lives with one of her adult children. She advises women to accept the way their children choose to spend their money, even if it does not meet with their approval, as long as the children continue to be financially stable. If, however, children spend beyond their means, the parent has the responsibility to give sage advice, albeit advice delivered respectfully.

This theme of women's respectful support is further evident in Brockman's advice to wives. In a digression from the topic of financial matters, Brockman moves to a discussion of wifely duties to an errant husband. If a husband looks beyond his wife, Brockman suggests: "Let us reflect on our own Demerit, and regulate what's in our power by a sincere Amendment: Let us learn by what Arts others engag'd him; but not forwardly upbraid him."[31] Obviously, Brockman places the blame for adultery upon a wife who cannot keep her husband's interests. She further explains, "never let us reprove such Faults directly, lest they construe it as a Saving to our selves; but rather shew them the ill-manners of it towards others."[32] During the 1650s, under the Puritans, adultery was made a capital offense, at least for women.[33] Often, adultery by men did not constitute a moral offense, let alone a legal one. Additionally, Thomas Heywood's *Curtain Lectures* (1637) addressed to bachelors and virgins concludes, "For a wife to beare with the weakness and imperfections of her husband is the true character of a wise and virtuous woman."[34] Brockman says much the same thing: "If he's a Brute [your husband], Good Humour supported with Virtue may other many Insinuations to help us keep possession."[35] In addition to responding to an errant husband with good humor, Brockman considers confronting a wayward husband directly is only a way of distracting attention from the wife's own faults in the matter—again the blame and responsibility rests upon the wife. The husband's transgression is only one of bad manners, and bad manners toward others, not his wife. Perhaps, financial dependency might explain Brockman's perspective: "Stock is united, and become one; the Husband has an unquestionable Command over that, as well as her Person."[36] Although Brockman does not explicitly link these two points, one point follows the other as if a social norm can be explained by a legal/financial one. Indeed, in a society where a wife's finances became her husband's upon marriage, and a husband was the legal guardian of his wife, acceptance of a husband's action was a financial and legal necessity.

As with child rearing, Brockman explains, one keeps a husband through good humor and mild behavior. Women must always be mild and in good humor for the benefit of the family: "if we can overcome our own resentment, the Conquest is near gain'd; for the teazing part, which blows the coal is removed from either side."[37] Notice that the husband is not required to do anything to keep the family together, but he is accepted absolutely. For, "there is hardly any cause, that can tolerate her being clamorous with a husband; If cannot mildly bring him to reason She must content her Self under the shelter of her Obedience."[38] Brockman reflects the dominant ideology concerning the role of women in the patriarchal culture. Steeped in a tradition of subservience and guilt perpetuated by the culture, women often considered this view perfectly normal, in fact, they might well have disputed any view that did not adhere to this ideology.

Although the first duty of wife was to her husband, being a mistress of a large estate entailed many more duties. Examining Renaissance books for women, Suzanne Hull discovered eighty-five practical guides, in 290 editions, that discussed housewifery. Frequently, housewifery involved supervising a sizable staff and included the role of a mentor and a doctor in a small community.[39] In Brockman's few letters, she displays a wifely and motherly concern for her family's health. Of the eight children born to her parents, Richard and Anne Glydd, only Anne and Martha survived to adulthood and her father died young. This persistent threat of childhood death is evident in Brockman's later life as well. Her eldest son, William, only twenty-eight, died during her lifetime. In a letter to her husband dated 1706, she is

> concerned for the illness at Longport, and more apprehensive for that it appears to be infectious, and my Dear I perceive is like to be very much in the danger of it, I wish you advise with Dr. Deeds for any preservatives for your self and family, and take the best care of your self as may be, and should you be any thing more then usually ill; I beg I may have the first notice of it, and I shall hasten to give what assistance I can.

Brockman adds, "my Mother gives her Blessing and is contriving many ways to invite you from the danger of infection." Anne Glydd Sr., although only a mother-in-law, also displays motherly concern. Apparently, Brockman remained close to her mother after her marriage to William, as evident from this entry: "I bless God we are all in health, I have twice walked to Pendhill."[40] Brockman lives close enough to her aging mother to continue her role as a good daughter.

Although Brockman mentions virtue seven times in her treatise, six are in general terms. She specifically mentions only one virtue: "the most general and ingaging Virtue that we can practise, is an extensive Charity in its proper sense,"[41] and she refers to the Bible passage 1 Corinthians 13 concerning charity. For Brockman, the proper sense of charity is not to squander money, to short ourselves, or to take from those who have just claim to the money. The proper sense of charity is sometimes a closed hand. Rather than opening a free financial hand to a prodigal son, Brockman cautions against lessons learned by too much charity. Brockman's vision of charity has a business attitude—correcting a need is a good investment and should profit all.

Brockman's third persona, the mistress of the house, reflects both her patrician status and her benevolence. Her treatise would probably have been read by her peers, upper-class women who were the mistresses of large estates with servants. Brockman's attitude toward servants suggests her attitude toward children, both require training without physical force. She does deviate on one important point between children and servants; she believes that servants are basically perverse and mischievous. Locke's attitude toward servants was much the same. He believed children learned bad language, tricks, and vice from "unbred or debauched" servants. Although Brockman does believe that the mistress must train her servants, she is not blamed if the training does not succeed. Brockman's general perspective on servants is that: "if servants were not so strangely perverse & mischievous, but would do their parts, they cou'd be easy, & do not enough." Although Brockman wishes that "there were less ground for this complaint," she believes that all servants fall within these bounds. It is the duty of the mistress to use "common prudence to regulate the overgrown height of servants." Brockman does blame the mistress of the house in one instance: "mistreses are deservedly blam'd, who have incouraged their [servant's] pride, falsely thinking their finery gives some reputation to their place & themselves; whereas this does but excite their Pride, which is the Root of all Vanity, destroying industry; Sloth follows . . ."[42] She believes that this instance allows for sloth and lack of respect for their "superiors." Brockman adheres to the belief that the upper class is the superior class, and since her primary readers were probably upper-class women, this argument would have addressed their concerns.

Although Brockman does recognize what she considers the innate defects of servants, she believes that they should not be treated badly. Like children, they should be shown the error of their ways, but it should be without being severe: "it's true we must sometimes chide & tell servants their faults, or they wou'd never know they did amiss; for we are not to expect so much ingenuity as that they shou'd correct themselves." Brockman not only believes that the mental capacity of a servant is childlike, but she also challenges the soundness of their thinking. Servants should be corrected in such a manner as to convince them of their faults while making them see how they could have done better, thus preventing any recurrence of their fault. Additionally, she believes that a show of anger by the mistress would be "likely to raise their savage passion" or provoke them to perform "some sort of revenge by carrying the crime still higher."[43] Obviously, servants are relegated to the same dimension as the savage. Brockman's English, upper-class background passes this judgment without any qualms about making the statements. She never tries to qualify such statements or to revise them to seem less superior. Brockman believes that emotion shown toward servants by the master or mistress could intensify their servants' childish and malicious personalities and raise their savage passions. As in the case of children, the use of "loud clamor" makes them fear "our thunder" and may occasion more faults, "overawing them will make fear, predominate & prevent free thinking," and chiding "for every fault, will have none mended."[44] Brockman suggests that servants who do not remedy their behavior should be released. She does make allowances for servants who are working to their ability but are still unable to perform to acceptable levels. Although much of Brockman's advice advocates a close relationship between child and parent, she opposes a close relationship between servant and mistress, because it lessens servants' respect for their superiors. Brockman contends that adult children should be viewed as equals to their parents, but she insists that servants should be treated as subordinates—they will never be equals. Brockman's attitude toward servants—inferior intellect, childish attitudes, excessive emotions or passions, fixation on pride, the need for constant supervision, and a general inferiority—mirrors some of the same attitudes men had toward women during this period.

In the few letters of Anne Brockman found in the British Library, the topic is often estate business—another role of the mistress when the master was away. According to Keith Wrightson, "many young gentlewomen acquired business sense as well as genteel accomplishments . . . an awareness of the essentials of estate management which they were expected to deploy at different stages of the life course."[45] Two letters to her husband, each dated 1718, discuss business, family and local gossip. The primary topic, the disposal of household goods for money, dominates both letters. On November 10, she writes,

> I am forward to answer your desire on my thoughts of disposing the things at Bletchingly [the Glydd family estate] and think it advisable all should be disposed on forthwith reserving only such linnen as is new or good of the kind for one use and sheets fit for our Servants beds and that pewter only as I formerly let by what else remains to be publickly sold and for the reserved linnen it should be carryed to Lond and so on to the

> green man at Bilingsgate and I believe we must give Niece Patty this aditionall trouble to the former.

Since Bletchingly County is the site of Pendhill, her mother's home, we can assume her mother has died, and Brockman must dispose of the estate. Two days later, Brockman reiterates these instructions to her husband, insuring that nothing in the estate is wasted. Further business is discussed as Brockman makes a deal for the wood on the family acreage, but awaits her husband's approval. The business tone of these letters is not one of mere reporting, but rather suggests understanding of estate business:

> they say they apprehend some trouble from a Lord, who lais clame to 2 acres of land call'd whitehill, I don't, but perhaps you may understand this story, we have at length got about 80 runts on the hill, but if they go of as quick at the next, as they did at last fair, we shall not have this prety prospect long.

Although Brockman does not entirely understand this particular incident (which she asks her husband to explain), she does understand the larger business it entails. Her command of estate finances is evident when she analyzes yearend profits based on current market trends. Furthermore, her confidence in her ability to run the estate in her husband's absence, coupled with her business acumen, qualifies her to discuss business with authority. In the estate business and in her private life, Brockman plans for the future.

What follows marriage and children, of course, is old age. Brockman explains, "There are scarce any who wish to die young to avoid the Infirmities of Age."[46] Brockman wrote *Age Rectified* at fifty-one, while Lady Sarah Cowper began her diary in her mid-fifties and often discussed her infirmities of aging. Unfortunately, those infirmities can necessitate living with one's children. Like Brockman, Cowper was concerned about her financial solvency in the event of widowhood. Even though her husband was in robust health, Cowper discussed her financial concerns with her husband. She worried about the rent after his death, and he assured her that he would leave orders that they should pay the rent. After his sudden death, her sons were not abiding to the terms of her settlement, and they refused to give her the cash for her rent and bills. To force her sons to financially support her, she showed them her diary and the entire text of the jointure settlement. Even though her diary was not a legal document, her son

William did pay her what was due that quarter.[47] As you can see, Brockman's fears were not unfounded. The financial status of widowhood could hinge on the adult children.

Although a house filled with three generations can be problematic, Brockman provides a blueprint for domestic bliss. Subservience is one element of senior skills for the dependent woman, but she also adds arbitration, medical knowledge, child care, teaching skills, and wisdom to raise the value of grandmother in the generational mix. Arbitration skills can be employed to ensure marital bliss for the head of household as exemplified in this advice: "Therefor we shou'd not appear to side with either, but in private persuade both to those things which are most reasonable, and may bring them nearest to Agreement: always remembering, that if it be not in a matter sinful, Condescension is the Woman's Duty."[48] Medical skill is valuable to the private woman to gain esteem within the family and her community: "if we have had opportunity to attain any competent Skill in Physick, or Surgery, this will be a useful Charity, that will gain us Esteem from the whole Neighbourhood."[49] A live-in babysitter is an asset to ingratiate both parents to the grandmother. An older woman can also play the role of a live-in tutor for moral issues in the household: "The catechizing, instructing and teaching of Children, is a Work of absolute necessity for their future well-being; and most commonly 'tis the Elders of the Family, that have the most leisure, and are best adapted to this useful Exercise." Silence is another virtue for a widow in her adult child's home:

> If from a sour Conversation and a thwarting Temper, we have it in our power to find a Remedy: if it be the strict Virtue, which will countenance nothing vicious or profane; let us be thankful to God, that he has given us such a distinguishing Qualification, which will enable us to take more pleasure in Heavenly Conversation, and make us less value worldly Enjoyments. Old People are commonly allow'd a decent Retirement; and we shou'd do well to be so provided, that it may not be irksom to us to be alone. This may be acquir'ed by sometimes using to withdraw when we might have Company, entertaining our selves with Books, the Pen, and such little Works, as sute with Age.[50]

Widowhood, even living within the family unit, can be a solitary existence. Providing for this existence includes preparation by learning skills to alleviate anxiety—primarily the anxiety of the younger generation. Learning both solitary and communal activities groom a woman for her final stage of life—old age. Brockman advises that women in "good Humour" are "generally esteem'd Benefits, and useful in their Generation."[51] Brockman's advice to help with the children, their education and health, to assist in community health, and to go about these duties joyfully can benefit the older woman by benefiting her family.

Essentially, a woman of any age is still valuable if she can continue to fulfill—and be defined by—the ideal of wife, mother, and mistress of the home—the caretaker of the family. Woman's identity was constructed within the context of her duties as mother and housewife, and "the old woman was a housewife without a household, a woman without a place."[52] When a widow lived with her adult child, she was an outsider. Having been the mistress of the house in the past, she was often seen as a potential threat to the present mistress of the house, her daughter-in-law. This unusual position within the household demanded a deft diplomacy to guarantee continued residence and financial support. Brockman's strategies straddle the abyss between the generations within the extended family unit. In this way, Brockman assures her readers that her advice will ensure domestic happiness: "altho we are not complemented now, true Worth will shine forth, and be valu'd in Life or Death; and 'tis a pleasing Reflection to think, our Memory shall smell sweet, when the Body putrifies."[53]

3

Age Rectified—The Edition

Ideas don't explode; they subvert. They take their time. And because they change the way we think, they are less visible than a newly paved national highway or the advent of wall-sized TVs. After a while, someone notices that we're not thinking about things the way our parents did.

Keith Hammonds, "Why the Net Really Changes Everything"[1]

Seen as an academic detective novel, this book can be divided into the following sections: the scene of the crime; that is, mother's advice books as a genre, demographics concerning wives, mothers, mistresses of the household, and aging women in seventeenth- and early eighteenth-century England; the suspect, the composite sketch of Lady Anne Brockman; the modus operandi, the authorship question; the corpse, *Age Rectified*; the evidence, the holograph, and the finger prints of the accomplices, the printer's marks; and the judgment—Lady Anne Brockman, guilty as charged—published author. Perhaps less lively than *The Thin Man* or *Law and Order*, it does, nevertheless, have the hallmark of a good mystery. The headlines should read: *Unknown author revealed after nearly four hundred years!* Buried in a mass grave of her family papers donated to the British Library, Brockman's text is finally exhumed, autopsied, and identified. But this tale is more than a mystery, it becomes a special case—a sourcebook of how the past is recreated from the perspective of the present.

Surprisingly, the research on Anne Brockman began with the well-examined play *Hamlet*. The "captain" of the research team of the *Hamlet Variorum*, Eric Rasmussen, gave the first clue to me, an academic sleuth. It led to a dark and dingy room and a simple listing of some women's writing found in the old British Library. The game was afoot, and a paper trail followed through two continents—the Brockman Family Papers in London, England; the ESTC microfilms in Reno, Nevada; and books of printing history, mother's advice books and criticism, cultural histories, the Drake-Brockman family history and demographics; and round again to the British Library, the first edition of *Age Rectified* and Kent, where I visited the Brockman tomb at St. Nicholas's Church and the family estate, Beachborourgh. Begun in 1996, the verdict of this mystery is the publication of this book.

This book presents the results of scholarly detection, highlighting the essentials of the investigation. Chapter 1 discusses seventeenth-century mother's advice books, and in turn, gives a background on some of the topics important to seventeenth-century Englishwomen. Although publication was usually a venue closed to women, motherhood seems to have provided a loophole to the ruling social ideal. In fact, authors of mother's advice books entered publishing through their private roles as mothers, who, unlike women in general, cannot be forced to remain silent if their entry into the public world of publication is to advise their children and other children by doing so. Chapter 2 discusses the suspected author. Little is known about her, but some information can be gleaned from the Brockman Papers at the British Library to understand who she was and what her advice book contained. Chapter 3 includes the investigation of authorship as well as the edition of *Age Rectified.*

Age Rectified and the Unknown Author

Included in the Brockman papers is an anonymous tract entitled "Age Rectified" in Anne Brockman's handwriting.[2] The British Library catalogue labels this holograph text as Anne Brockman's laborious copy of the published treatise, *Age Rectified*,[3] that is, as her painstaking, word-by-word reproduction of the anonymously published treatise. First published in 1709, *Age Rectified* was reprinted in 1742, suggesting its continuing influence across almost half a century. Although the printed tract describes the author only as: "One of the Same Sex," many notations on the Brockman holograph (handwritten manuscript) supply evidence that it is *not* a copy of the printed text, but quite the reverse—that is, the holograph manuscript is the draft for the printed one.

During the Renaissance and early eighteenth century, copying printed texts by hand was a common occurrence. As a rule, however, texts were copied when the printed ones were unavailable or when they were too expensive for the budget. Neither of these reasons applies to Anne Brockman; William Brockman was often in London, where *Age Rectified* was printed, and the Brockmans, landed gentry with large holdings, could afford to purchase the book. Moreover, the holograph is thirty-one pages long—no small copying task. Essentially, it does not make sense for Anne Brockman, mistress of a large estate, to spend time copying a text she could easily buy. In addition to this objection of Brockman as copier, there are notations within the holograph that point toward corrections made by a printer or compositor.

Marked signatures, page breaks, consistent spelling corrections, and sentence-level editing in a hand other than Brockman's all suggest a printer or compositor correcting the holograph in preparation for printing. Research on printing practices in the time period suggest that authors' holographs were used as the basis for the printing, although compositors often corrected the text for printing and then returned the original to the author.[4] The notations found in the margins and within the Brockman holography indicate a corrected draft, rather than a copy.

Before the discussion about printers' or compositors' notations begins, some background about bookmaking is necessary. Book text is printed on a large sheet of paper that includes many book pages on both sides of the one large sheet of paper.[5] This sheet is then folded and cut to form a smaller sheet that contains the pages of a book. The sheet—printed, folded, and cut—is then combined into a group of pages called a signature or gathering (this folded sheet will be referred to as a gathering throughout this discussion). Each page includes page numbers, but in addition, some of the pages also have a letter and number combination assigned to them, called a signature, that would indicate the gathering or group of pages (figure 3.1). The first gathering is designated as the "A-gathering," and an "A" would appear on the first page—the right-hand or recto page. This would continue through the alphabet and repeat with double letters for larger books. The signature on each gathering or group of pages allows the printer

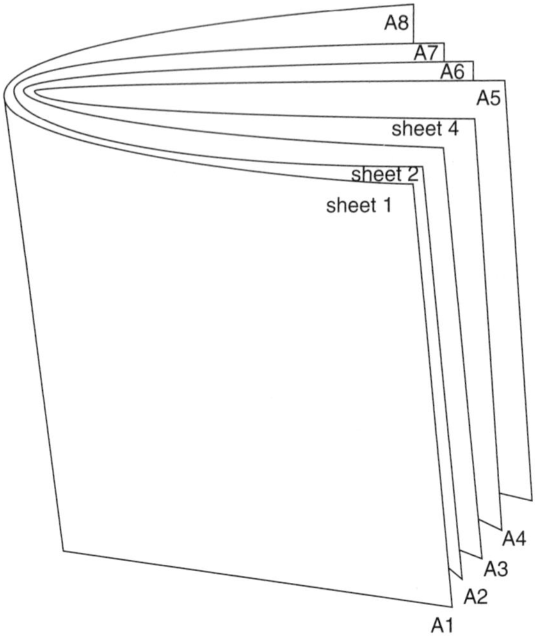

Figure 3.1 Illustration of a gathering, drawn by Marsha Urban.

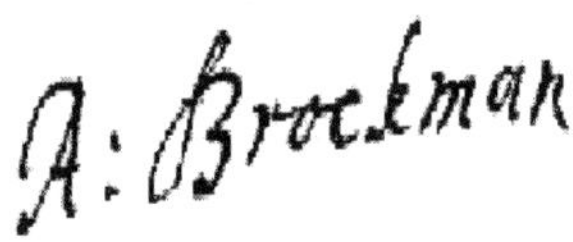

Figure 3.2 Anne Brockman's signature. Holograph, the Brockman Papers, the British Library, ADD. 42587, dated 1706.

to place each gathering in the correct succession quickly, "A" gathering through to the last alphabetical gatherings. Once the gatherings are grouped, the pages can be bound to make the finished book, as shown above.[6]

The Brockman holograph contains numerous signature notations. On page eight of the handwritten manuscript, the A12 signature appears in the margin. The "A" is not in Brockman's handwriting (Brockman's signature, figure 3.2). Also, this signature marks the twelfth page of the A-gathering. This notation is absent from the

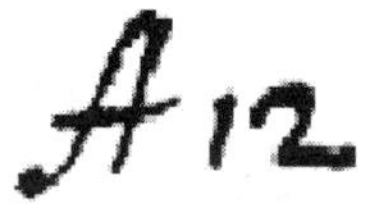

Figure 3.3 A12 signature. Holograph, the Brockman Papers, the British Library, ADD. 42611, dated 1709.

Figure 3.4 B-gathering signature. Holograph, the Brockman Papers, the British Library, ADD. 42611, dated 1709.

Figure 3.5 B14 signature. Holograph, the Brockman Papers, the British Library, ADD. 42611, dated 1709.

printed text (figure 3.3). Had Brockman been copying the printed text, marking the A12 signature would necessitate counting each page of the A-gathering to determine the twelfth. When someone copies a printed text, counting pages of a gathering would be pointless, because the page numbers appear on each page of the printed text, and the signature is not needed to keep your place in the text.

Another signature notation can be found on page thirteen of the Brockman holograph. This notation is common marking for the beginning of a gathering, in this case, the B-gathering (figure 3.4). Included in this notation is the number of the page from the printed text, page seventeen. Both Percy Simpson, a twentieth-century scholar and Joseph Moxon, a seventeenth-century expert in the field of print-making, believe that compositors ticked off the pages as they finished, and these marks do, in effect, tick off the pages.[7] In this instance the signature "B" does appear in the printed text to signal the new fold. As in the A12 signature, a B14 appears in the margins of the holograph, page twenty-five (figure 3.5). And like the A12 signature, this notation does not appear in the printed version; one must count the pages of the

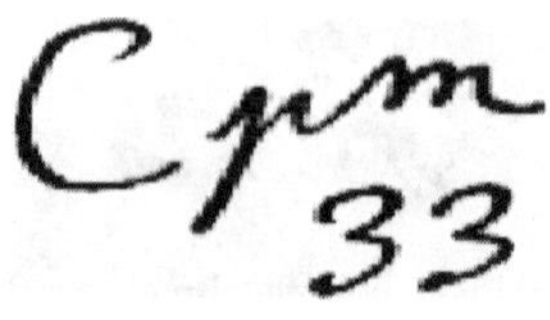

Figure 3.6 C signature. Holograph, the Brockman Papers, the British Library, ADD. 42611, dated 1709.

Figure 3.7 Jealousy page break. Holograph, the Brockman Papers, the British Library, ADD. 42611, dated 1709.

B-gathering to arrive at B14. Moreover, the "B" is not in Brockman's usual hand.

The last signature notation can be found in the margins of page twenty-eight in the Brockman manuscript. This is also the beginning of the C-gathering, and it contains the page number of the printed text thirty-three. The "C" and page number does appear in the printed text, but the notation that designates it as the beginning of a gathering does not (figure 3.6). In addition to the signatures, there are small numbers in the margin of the holograph that indicate where the printed page ends. An example is a small thirteen of the printed text, but found on page ten of the holograph. The approximate location of the thirteen on page ten of the holograph roughly indicates the end of page thirteen of the text. This marginal notation ends on page sixteen and is replaced with two horizontal lines, a common compositors' notation for the end of a fold, marking the end of page seventeen and the beginning of the B-gathering. The B-gathering numbering resumes with two and runs through sixteen, marking the pages of the B-gathering. The horizontal lines mark the end of page thirty-three and the beginning of the C-gathering. Again, these notations correlate with Moxon's and Simpsons' description of printer practices.

There are also five exact page breaks identified in the manuscript by square brackets, a common compositors' mark. Four of the five page breaks occur at the beginning of a word, but the page break on page twelve of the printed text breaks a word—jealousy (figure 3.7). This break appears on page twelve of Brockman's holograph at the exact spot where the printed page ends. In the four other instances, brackets appear in the Brockman's holograph before the word that begins the new page. Although square brackets are a common form of compositors' notation for a page break, it would not be common to anyone else. Moreover, square brackets do not appear anywhere in the printed text.

In addition to the technical notations for page breaks and signatures, the Brockman holograph includes sentence-level editing as well. During this time, printers used their own "rough and ready system" of spelling.[8] Throughout the Brockman handwritten manuscript, spelling is corrected in a handwriting other than Brockman's. Correcting Brockman's normal "bin" to "been" repeats throughout. In Brockman's letters, she uses "bin" exclusively. If she did copy the printed text, there is a possibility that she would follow its use of the "been" spelling. Even if she did not copy "been," there is no reason why she would go through her copy to correct such common words for spelling irregularities, especially when the corrected spelling is the one she preferred. Additionally, her use of a double "l" (awefull) or a single "e" (coale) at the end of words is also corrected. Both endings, common to Brockman, do not affect the pronounciation of the words. Further, "remidy" is corrected to "remedy." With only a vowel change in the spelling of "remedy," and a vowel that can easily be read either way, correcting this word does not warrant extra work. Only a compositor who is preparing a proof for the printsetter would bother with such a small change.[9] Also, it was compositors who changed spellings for consistency throughout the text.

The manuscript also includes editing on the sentence level. In this case this change is in Brockman's own hand, as shown on page two of the manuscript (figure 3.8). But the other corrections—adding words, taking words out, and in one case changing an entire sentence—have

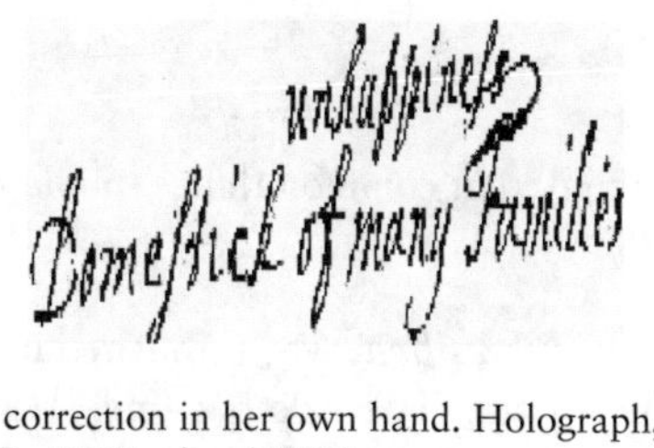

Figure 3.8 Brockman correction in her own hand. Holograph, the Brockman Papers, the British Library, ADD. 42611, dated 1709.

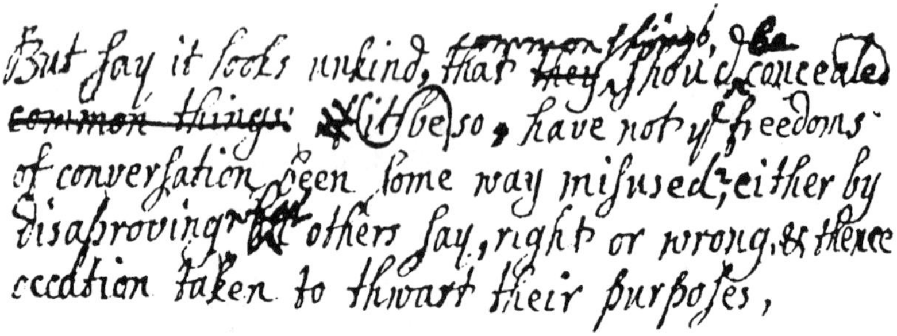
But say it looks unkind, that common things, they shou'd conceale common things: if it be so, have not ye freedoms of conversation been some way misused; either by disaproving what others say, right or wrong, & thence occation taken to thwart their purposes,

Figure 3.9 Corrections by another hand in the Brockman holograph. Holograph, The Brockman Papers, the British Library, ADD. 42611, dated 1709.

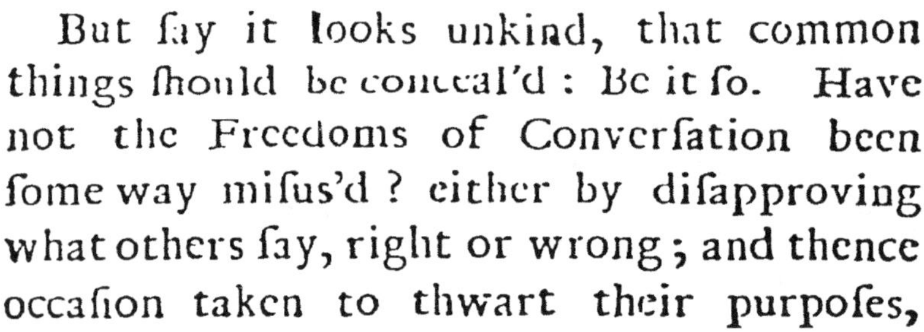
But ſay it looks unkind, that common things ſhould be conceal'd: Be it ſo. Have not the Freedoms of Converſation been ſome way miſus'd? either by diſapproving what others ſay, right or wrong; and thence occaſion taken to thwart their purpoſes,

Figure 3.10 *Age Rectified*. Holograph, the Brockman Papers, the British Library, ADD. 42611, dated 1709.

been made in a hand other than Brockman's. The corrections in the other hand, which appear on the manuscript, then appear in the printed text (figure 3.9). The number of corrections in this sentence surely indicates not mistakes but deliberate editing of Brockman's manuscript:

> But say it looks unkind, that they shou'd conceale common things: if it be so,
>
> <u>changed to:</u>
>
> But say it looks unkind, that common things should be conceal'd: Be it so (see figure 3.10).

A new edition of *Age Rectified*, was published in 1747 (figure 3.11), changing only the title page. The title became: *AGE made HAPPY as well as HONOURABLE, by a Select Number of CAUTIONARY*

RULES, for the Rendering of it Equally Pleasing both to Ourselves and Others, instead of being OBNOXIOUS to BOTH. The title page, with this atrociously long title (but typical of the time), also designates the audience: "Seriously Recommended to Persons of all Ranks," and identifies a new author: "compiled by a lady of great quality for the use of herself and family." Anne Brockman had been dead for seventeen years when the second edition was published. In 1709, Brockman connected with her audience through gender (figure 3.12). The holograph title page also makes this connection (figure 3.13). She designates her audience as women, serious matrons and defines herself as "one of the same sex." The 1747 edition is more inclusive, but more class conscious. The later edition includes all ranks, but specifically designates the author as "a lady of great quality." Indeed, Lady Anne Brockman, mistress of a great manor house and heiress to one well-known name and married into another, Glydd and Brockman, was a lady of "great quality."

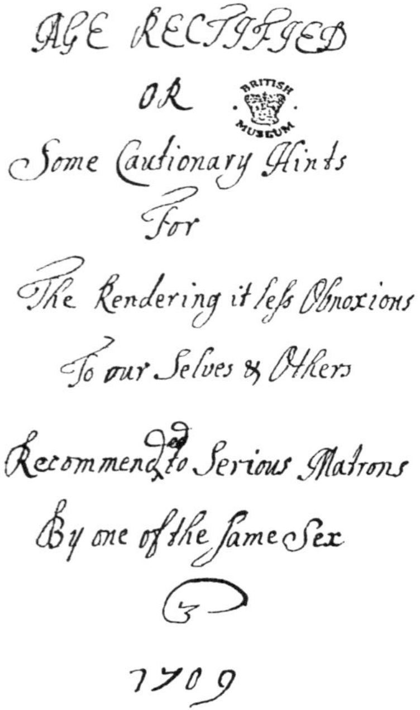

AGE RECTIFIED
OR
Some Cautionary Hints
For
The Rendering it leſs Obnoxious
To our Selves & Others
Recommended to Serious Matrons
By one of the ſame Sex
1709

Figure 3.11 Title page, Brockman holograph of *Age Rectified*. Holograph, the Brockman Papers, the British Library, ADD. 42611, dated 1709.

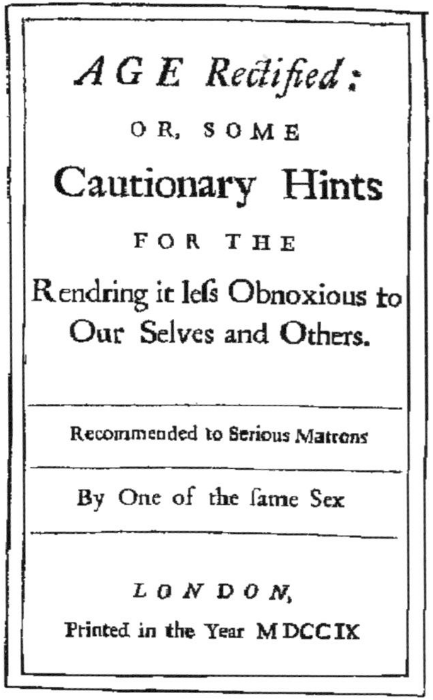

AGE Rectified:
OR, SOME
Cautionary Hints
FOR THE
Rendring it leſs Obnoxious to Our Selves and Others.

Recommended to Serious Matrons

By One of the ſame Sex

LONDON,
Printed in the Year MDCCIX

Figure 3.12 *Age Rectified*, printed title page. *Age Rectified*. London, 1709. 20.

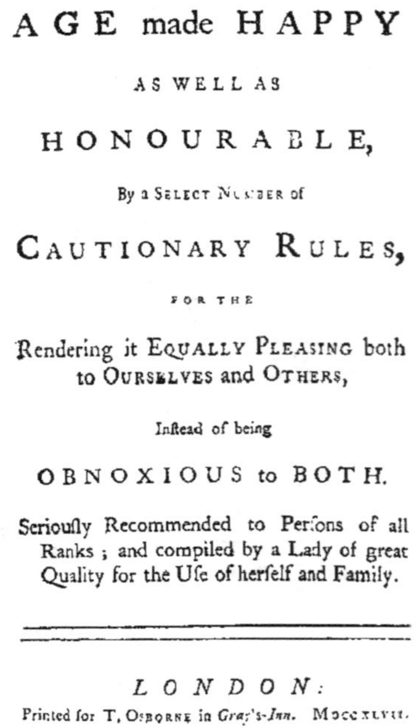

AGE made HAPPY
AS WELL AS
HONOURABLE,
By a SELECT NUMBER of
CAUTIONARY RULES,
FOR THE
Rendering it EQUALLY PLEASING both to OURSELVES and OTHERS,
Inſtead of being
OBNOXIOUS to BOTH.
Seriouſly Recommended to Perſons of all Ranks; and compiled by a Lady of great Quality for the Uſe of herſelf and Family.

LONDON:
Printed for T. OSBORNE in *Gray's-Inn.* MDCCXLVII.

Figure 3.13 *Age Made Happy*, title page, 1742.

Age Rectified—The Edition

This edition contains the holograph or handwritten manuscript on the left page and the text of the published treatise on the facing page. The published treatise has been divided to match the lines of the manuscript. This format allows for comparison of the manuscript, with printer's marginal notes, and the editing that appeared in the text. To further facilitate this comparison, the lines of the printed text mirror the manuscript lines, and all page breaks and signatures that appear in the printed text are added. This paralleling of the texts highlights the fact that corrections made on the manuscript appear in the printed text. Figure 3.14 shows the first page of the manuscript and the first page of the printed text.

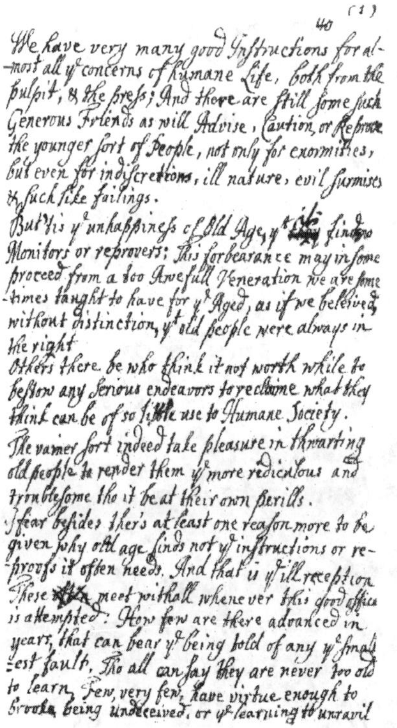

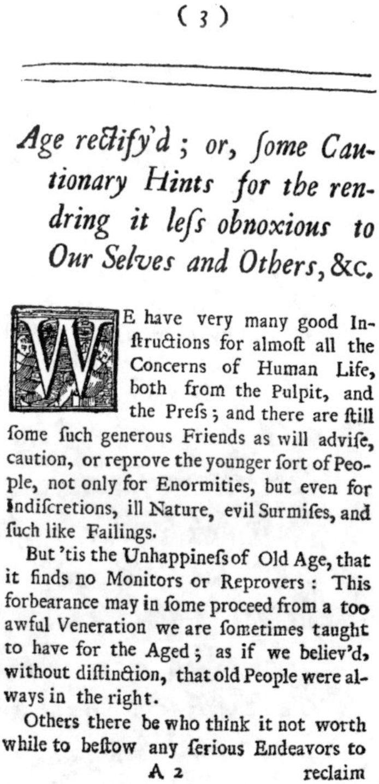

(3)

Age rectify'd ; or, ſome Cautionary Hints for the rendring it leſs obnoxious to Our Selves and Others, &c.

WE have very many good Inſtructions for almoſt all the Concerns of Human Life, both from the Pulpit, and the Preſs ; and there are ſtill ſome ſuch generous Friends as will adviſe, caution, or reprove the younger ſort of People, not only for Enormities, but even for Indiſcretions, ill Nature, evil Surmiſes, and ſuch like Failings.

But 'tis the Unhappineſs of Old Age, that it finds no Monitors or Reprovers : This forbearance may in ſome proceed from a too awful Veneration we are ſometimes taught to have for the Aged ; as if we believ'd, without diſtinction, that old People were always in the right.

Others there be who think it not worth while to beſtow any ſerious Endeavors to

A 2 reclaim

Figure 3.14 *Age Rectified* first page of manuscript and printed text.

Age Rectified, the edition. Holograph, the Brockman Papers, the British Library, ADD. 42611, dated 1709.

(1)

40

We have very many good Instructions for al-most all ye concerns of Humane Life, both from the Pulpit, & the Press; And there are still some such Generous Friends as will Advise, Caution, or Reprove the younger sort of People, not only for enormities, but even for indiscretions, ill nature, evil surmises & such like failings.

But 'tis ye unhappiness of Old Age, yt [illegible] finds no Monitors or reprovers; This forbearance may in some proceed from a too Awefull Veneration we are some-times taught to have for ye Aged, as if we believed, without distinction, yt old people were always in the right

Others there be who think it not worth while to bestow any Serious endeavors to reclaime what they think can be of so little use to Humane Society.

The vainer sort indeed take pleasure in thwarting old people to render them ye more ridiculous and troublesome tho it be at their own perills.

I fear besides ther's at least one reason more to be given why old age finds not ye instructions or re-proofs it often needs. And that is ye ill reception These [illegible] meet withall whenever this good office is attempted: How few are there advanced in years, that can bear ye being told of any ye small-est fault, Tho all can say they are never too old to learn. Few, very few, have virtue enough to brook being undeceived, or ye learning to unravil

We have very many good Instructions for almost all the Concerns of Human Life, both from the Pulpit, and the Press; and there are still some such generous Friends as will advise, caution, or reprove the younger sort of People, not only for Enormities, but even for Indiscretions, ill Nature, evil Surmises, and such like Failings.

But 'tis the Unhappiness of Old Age, that it finds no Monitors or Reprovers: This forbearance may in some proceed from a too awful Veneration we are some times taught to have for the Aged; as if we beleiv'd, without distinction, that old People were always in the right.

Others there be who think it not worth while to bestow any serious Endeavors to [A2] [pp 4] reclaim what they think can be of so little use to Human Society.

The vainer sort indeed take pleasure in thwarting old People, to render them the more ridiculous and troublesom, tho it be at their own Peril.

I fear besides, there's at least one reason more to be given why old Age finds not the Instructions or Reproofs it often needs: And that is the ill reception these meet withal whenever this good Office is attempted. How few are there advanc'd in years, that can bear the being told of any the smallest fault, tho all can say they are never too old to learn? Few, very few, have Virtue enough to brook[10] being undeceiv'd, of the Learning to unravel

Age Rectified, the edition. Holograph, the Brockman Papers, the British Library, ADD. 42611, dated 1709.

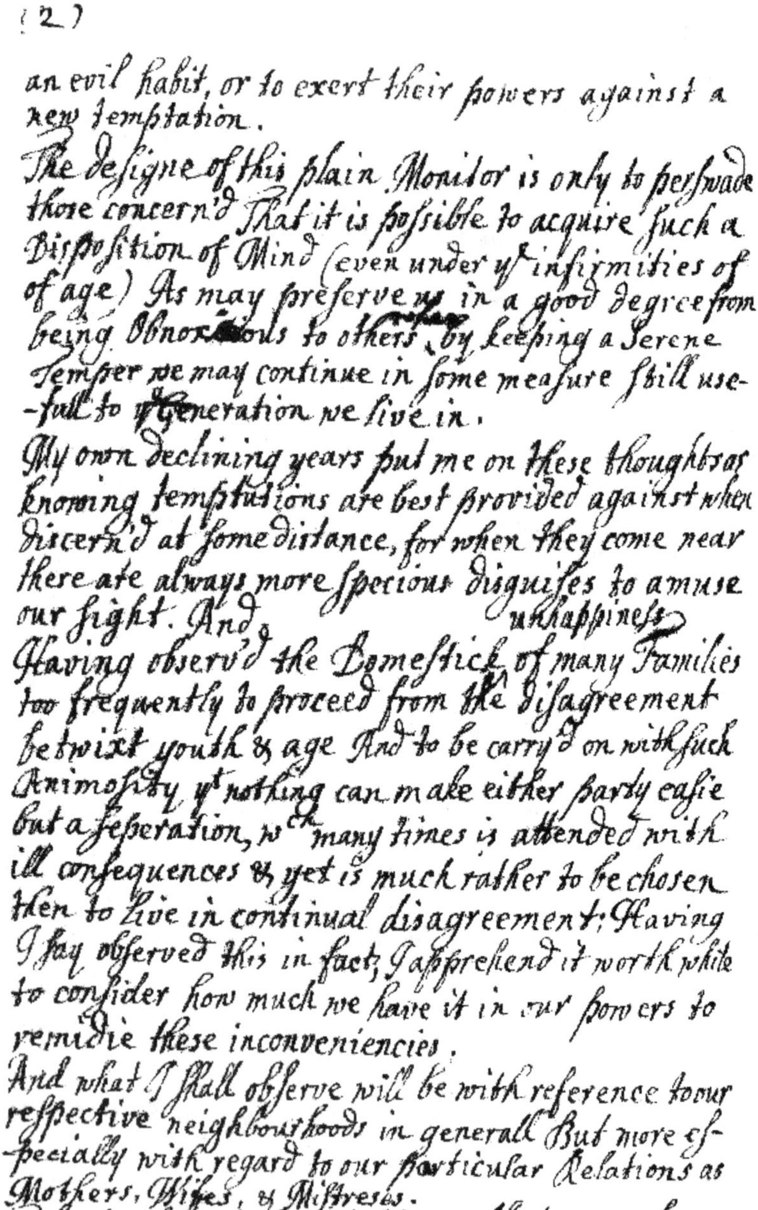

(2)

an evil habit, or to exert their powers against a new temptation.

The designe of this plain Monitor is only to perswade those concern'd That it is possible to acquire such a Disposition of Mind (even under ye infirmities of of age) As may preserve us in a good degree from being Obnoxious to others, by keeping a Serene Temper we may continue in some measure still use-full to ye Generation we live in.

My own declining years put me on these thoughts as knowing temptations are best provided against when discern'd at some distance, for when they come near there are always more specious disguises to amuse our sight. And

Having observ'd the Domestick unhappiness of many Families too frequently to proceed from the disagreement betwixt youth & age And to be carry'd on with such Animosity yt nothing can make either party easie but a seperation, wch many times is attended with ill consequences & yet is much rather to be chosen then to live in continual disagreement; Having I say observed this in fact, I apprehend it worth while to consider how much we have it in our powers to remidie these inconveniencies.

And what I shall observe will be with reference to our respective neighbourhoods in generall But more es-pecially with regard to our particular Relations as Mothers, Wifes, & Mistreses.

begin then at the root let us reflect on our former

an evil Habit, or to exert their Powers against a new Temptation.

The Design of this plain Monitor is only to persuade those concern'd, that it is possible to acquire such a Disposition of Mind (even under the Infirmities of Age) as may preserve us in a good degree from being obnoxious to others; when by keeping a serene Temper we may continue in some measure still useful to the Generation we live in.

My own declining Years put me on these Thoughts, as knowing Temptations are best provided against when discern'd at some distance; for when they come near, there are **[A3] [pp 5]** always more specious Disguises to amuse our Sight. And,

Having observ'd the Domestick Unhappiness of many Families too frequently to proceed from the disagreement betwixt Youth and Age, and to be carry'd on with such Animosity, that nothing can make either Party easy but a Separation,[11] which many times is attended with ill Consequences, and yet is much rather to be chosen than to live in continual Disagreement: Having, I say, observ'd this in Fact, I apprehend it worth while to consider how much we have it in our Power to remedy these Inconveniences.

And what I shall observe will be with reference to our respective Neighbourhoods in general, but more especially with regard to our particular Relations, as Mothers, Wives, and Mistresses.

To begin then at the root, let us reflect on our former

(3)

Conduct in order to ye making sutable reparations for what has been a-miss.
Have we carry'd a very severe hand over our Children not only to restrain them from evil (for so much its certainly every on's duty to do) But even to keep ym at an awfull distance, making ym dread our dis-pleasure for every childish fault, Allowing ym little familiarity in our company, loading ym with commands out of pleasure to see our selves obey'd without regarding ye benefit of those we command Or have abated of this rigor as their reason & know-ledge increased for these ought to be imploy'd & preferr'd as much ye fitest instruments to profit ym withal. Which shou'd be a Parents main designe; For if we carry on severities to yt age when they may reasonably expect to be free, & set up some sort of government of themselves & others, we have little reason reason to wonder they shou'd desire to shake us off. Tis very hard for free born Rationals to live always under awfull checks & restraint.
And I doubt it is also hard for such to give up the beloved government, who have not considered for what end it was given ym, & how long to be continued Government is here only to be used for ye Benefit of ye governed; with watchfull discipline we are to train ym up in ye way yt they shou'd goe & when they come to years of Discretion we hope

Conduct, in order to the making sutable Reparations for what has been amiss.

Have we carry'd a very severe hand over our Children, not only to restrain them from evil (for so much it's certainly every one's Duty to do) but even to keep them at an awful distance, making them dread our Displeasure for every childish fault, allowing them little familiarity in our Company, **[pp 6]** loading them with Commands, out of pleasure to see our selves obey'd, without regarding the benefit of those we command? Or have we abated of this rigor, as their Reason and Knowledg increas'd? for these ought to be imploy'd and prefer'd, as much the fittest Instruments to profit them withal. Which shou'd be a Parent's main Design; for if we carry on Severities to that Age when they may reasonably expect to be free, and set up some sort of Government of themselves and others, we have little reason to wonder they shou'd desire to shake us off. 'Tis very hard for freeborn Rationals to live always under awful Checks and Restraint.[12]

And I doubt it also hard for such to give up the beloved Government, who have not consider'd for what end it was given them, and how long to be continu'd. Government is here only to be us'd for the Benefit of the Govern'd: with watchful Discipline we are to train them up in the way that they shou'd go; and when they come to years of Discretion, we hope

(4)
They will not depart from it; However severity can then be of little use: For that will only make y^m more industrious to conceal their faults, or else to shun & avoid our company & so put themselves out of ye way of being reclaim'd by our friendly Advice, good Example, & handsome Insinuations, wch might take some hold of them in proper seasons, if we did contain our anger, or vent it rather at ye like Crimes in other persons, as occation offers, And enlarging most upon ye ill consequences of evil courses, we may condemn facts with such tender regard to Persons as may manifest our goodwill towards them. If there be much gall in our anger ye whole subject of it will be thought to proceed from our own peevish humour rather then from any Principle of Virtue & so finde but little regard. Where good Education has not bin wanting, I am willing to believe there needs nothing But good humour with a few cautions on both sides, to make reciprocal Indearments betwixt Parents & Children.

Has there been too much severity towards y^m in youth there must be ye more indulgence shewn when grown up, to convince y^m that we did it only to bring y^m to ye knowledg of themselves & to the obedience due to a Supream Power, whose Commands as dictated by ye Holy Scriptures &

they will not depart from it. However, Severity can then be of little use: For that will only make them more industrious to conceal their faults, or else to shun and avoid our Company, and so put themselves out of the way of being reclaim'd by our friendly Advice, good Example, and [**pp** 7] handsom Insinuation; which might take some hold of them in proper Season, if we did contain our Anger, or vent it rather at the like Crimes in other Persons, as occasion offers: and enlarging most upon the ill Consequences of evil Courses, we may condemn Facts with such tender regard to Persons, as may manifest our good Will towards them. If there be much Gall in our Anger, the whole Subject of it will be thought to proceed from our own peevish Humour, rather than from any Principle of Virtue, and so find but little regard.[13]

Where good Education has not been wanting, I am willing to believe there needs nothing, but good Humour, with a few Cautions on both sides, to make reciprocal Indearments betwixt Parents and Children.

Has there been too much Severity towards them in Youth? there must be the more Indulgence shewn when grown up, to convince them that we did it only to bring them to the knowledg of themselves, and to the obedience due to a Supreme Power; whose Commands, as dictated by the Holy Scriptures, and

(5) +2 (5)

Their own Conscience they must most strictly
observe to their lives end.
Some Parents there are, who either by a total neg-
-lect of their Children, or leaving them wholy to
7 others tuition, give no occation for complaints of
this kind, And yet they are angry, yt when they are
grown up they are not what they cou'd wish them
I know nothing yt can excuse Parents from takeing
some part in forming their minds at least in their
tender years when some Happy impressions may
be made; Then even their necessityes, who labour
for bread, may allow some Leisure for this so ne-
-cessary work.
But I doubt it is often such as have most leisure
that least care to set about this business, thinking
it will give interruption to their company, & di-
-vertions; how just then is it that in years they
shou'd retaliate this Usage. This reflection should
move us to seek pleasure in conversing with our
children & seeking we shall surely find it. By
considering their improvements are owing to our
labour; And we shall so distinctly discern their
tempers as to know how ye better to dispose other
occurrences of life, It is not my purpose to enlarge
on this usefull theme. But for such as have bin
of this careless sort I know of no better Expedient
at present then to bribe their childrens love with
benefits: till by a more prudent Conduct they

their own Conscience, they must strictly
observe to their Lives end.

Some Parents there are, who either by a total neglect of their Children, or leaving them wholly to others Tuition, give no **[A4]** **[PP 8]** occasion for Complaints of this kind; and yet they are angry, that when they are grown up, then are not what they cou'd wish them.

I know nothing that can excuse Parents from taking some part in forming their Minds, at least in their tender years, when some happy Impressions may be made; then even their Necessitys, who labour for Bread, may allow some leisure for this so necessary Work.

But I doubt it is often such as have most leisure that least care to set bout this Business, thinking it will give interruption to their Company, and Diversions. How just then is it that in years they Shou'd retaliate this Usage? This Reflection should move us to seek pleasure in conversing with our Children; and seeking we shall surely find it, by considering their Improvements are owing to our Labour: and we shall so distinctly discern their Tempers, as to know how the better to dispose other Occurrences of Life. It is not my purpose to inlarge on this useful Theme. But for such as have been of this careless sort, I know no better Expedient at present, than to bribe their Childrens Love with Benefits; till by a more prudent Conduct they

(6)
acquire such a habit as may lay a better foundati-
-on for a good understanding betwixt me & the other.
There is yet an other sort of Parents who through
an inconsiderate fondness have Indulged their
children in all their craving desires, wch undoubted-
-ly will increase with years till they can go no
farther, And how then will such Parents keep
peace with them, whom they can no longer Oblige; when
These understand not any better arguments of love
Truly this will prove a difficulty, The best method
I can think of is, That such turn ye scale upon
them, telling ym, that they Indulg'd their tender
years to bring them to maturity, And now yt they
are in their full Strength & your selves declining
you expect ye like observance from them.
If they dont relish this change, take courage & try
to withdraw yr Self from ym for a while, Or put
them from you where they may meet with some
difficultyes & not be so much humoured (do this
at least for a weaning) And then begin again
with no other civilities, then it's common for
one friend in familiarity to pay an other, Expect
-ing the like return from them: For under this
character I wou'd have both Parents, & Children,
esteem each other, Taking the Obligation of Friend-
-ship to be much more Engaging then yt of Parentall
Duty when Children are come to years of Discretion.

acquire such a Habit, as may lay a better foundation for a good Understanding betwixt one and the other. **[PP 9]** There is yet another sort of Parents, who thro an inconsiderate fondness have indulg'd their Children in all their craving Desires, which undoubtedly will increase with years, till they can go no farther. And how then will such Parents keep Peace with them whom they can no longer oblige? When these understand not any better Arguments of Love, truly this will prove a difficulty. The best Method I can think of, is, That such turn the Scale upon them, telling them, that they indulg'd their tender years to bring them to Maturity; and now that they are in their full Strength, and your selves declining, you expect the like observance from them.

If they don't relish this Change, take Courage, and try to withdraw your self from them for a while; or put them from you, where they may meet with some Difficultys, and not be so much humour'd (do this at least for a weaning) and then begin again with no other Civilities, than it's common for one Friend in familiarity to pay another, expecting the like return from them: For under this Character I wou'd have both Parents, and Children, esteem each other; taking the Obligation of Friendship to be much more engaging than that of Parental Duty, when Children are come to years of Discretion.

(7)

I beleive it the occation of great disappoyntments
& uneasiness, That Parents expect their Children
shou'd pay them an observance almost to Adorati-
-on when grown up, tho perhaps they owe little more
to them than their birth, & such a provision as ye
[illegible] inforceth, as if they were given only for
our behoofe & not rather we appoynted as guard-
-ans to take care of them.
But indeed if kind Parents live to ye decay of
their bodily strength & Reason, so far yt they can-
-not decently support themselves, Children have
then ye utmost obligation to do for, & bear with,
them, Remembering how long, & with what ten-
-derness they were taken care of in their like
feeble State; In Gods designe of Government the
stronger are still to assist the weaker; mere
nature wou'd teach us this duty if we were so
happy as to make reason our rule.
The ground most commonly disputed is when we
stand nearest on a level; for so I call it when
young ones enter upon business for themselves, or
lay foundations for families, we ought not then
violently to oppose their fixt inclinations: unless
there be something in it evidently pernicious; tho
calme reasoning is never to be omitted, setting
before their eyes good, & evil consequences, accord
ing to the nature of things. For we are now

[PP 10] I believe it the occasion of great Disappointments and Uneasiness, That Parents expect their Children shou'd pay them an Observance almost to Adoration when grown up, tho perhaps they owe little more to them than their Birth, and such a Provision as the Law inforceth: as if they were given only for our behoof,[14] and not rather we appointed as Guardians to take care of them.

But indeed if kind Parents live to the decay of their bodily Strength and Reason, so far that they cannot decently support themselves, Children have then the utmost Obligation to do for, and bear with, them; remembring how long, and with what Tenderness they were taken care of in their like feeble State. In God's Design of Government, the Stronger are still to assist the Weaker: Mere Nature wou'd teach us this Duty, if we were so happy as to make Reason our Rule.

The Ground most commonly disputed is when we stand nearest on a level; for so I call it when Young Ones enter upon Business for themselves, or lay Foundations for Families: we ought not then violently to oppose their fixt Inclinations, unless there be something in it evidently pernicious; tho calm reasoning is never to be omitted, setting before their Eyes good and evil **[PP 11]**Consequences, according to the nature of things. For we are now

(8)
no longer to look upon them as our inferiors
but may assuredly esteem them our Equals, with
the only reserve of Precedency; if we do not, others
will, The World being disposed rather to adore the
rising, then ye Setting, Sun: It is a very Gratefull
Honour to both; when children are said to inherit
the virtues of their Parents.
It would certainly conduce more to the happyness of Life
did Mankind all think themselves members of
one Body, tho not all fitted for ye same use, nor
in the same degree of Honour, Yet all concern'd
to carry on the proper Benefit of the whole in
every individial part
Then shou'd we not fret & teaze one-an-other
for things of small moment; These are ye evils
I wou'd prevent, Which creep into our veins
unwarily lie unseen like vipers in the grass,
but send poisonous fumes to ye head, that fall
in foggy vapors on ye mind, And both good
humour, & good judgment, are in danger of be-
-ing lost in such a mist: In great troubles, wch
are visible to by-standers, consolatory Friends
help bear a part of ye burthen, And time effec-
-tually lessens it. But if we have suffered our-
-selves to be corrupted with Jealousy, Distrust, A 12
Heartburnings, evil Surmises, Peevish Discontent,
& Slanderous backbitings, These are our own offspring

no longer to look upon them as our inferiors but may assuredly esteem them our Equals, with the only reserve of Precedency;[15] if we do not, others will, the World being dispos'd rather to adore the rising, than the setting, Sun. It is a very grateful Honour to both, when Children are said to inherit the Virtues of their Parents.

It would certainly conduce more to Happiness of Life, did Mankind all think themselves Members of one Body, tho not all fitted for the same use, nor in the same degree of Honour; yet all concern'd to carry on the proper Benefit of the Whole in every individual Part.[16]

Then should we not fret and teaze one another for things of small moment. These are the Evils I wou'd prevent, which creep into our Veins unwarily, lie unseen like Vipers in the Grass, but send poisonous Fumes to Head, that fall in foggy Vapours on the Mind; and both good Humour, and good Judgment, are in danger of being lost in such mist. In great Troubles, which are visible to By-Standers, consolatory Friends help bear a part of the Burden, and time effectually lessens it. But if we have suffer'd ourselves to be corrupted with **[PP 12]** Jealousy, Distrust, Heart-burnings, evil Surmises, peevish Discontent, and slanderous Back-bitings; these are our own offspring,

(9)

And the Cure lies chiefly in our own Breast, for
others will bring fuell, blow ye coals, & keep feed
-ing the fire, seeming to humour us, but rather
to gratifie some humour of their own, giving
themselves & others diversion with ye mischief
they make.

And it's ten to one but there's some old depending
Servant, Nurse, or Neighbour, that thinks to
ingratiate themselves into our favour by whis-
-pering in our ear after this manner
Ah Good Lady ye world does not go now as it did
in our younger days, we were not wont to have
it at this pass when I first knew you, nor need
it be so now if things were well manag'd, but
young folks will not be advised, nobody regards
what we old folk say, with many more such like
incentives.

But Let us Consider whither any thing of this kind
be worth hearkning to. The World is still ye same,
& will be to ye worlds end, Tho modes, & manners,
alter yearly; most things are upon ye improvement;
12 we see Arts, & Sciences, increase daily, Ornament-
-all Ingenuity is more conspicuous in every degree,
I see nothing that's wanting in generall but
Truth & Honesty, & I heartily wish there were
more than wou'd help cultivate these, in their own
Nature, Universall Benefits; yet Soloman bids us

and the Cure lies chiefly in our own Breast: For others will bring Fuel, blow the Coals, and keep feeding the Fire; seeming to humour us, but rather to gratify some Humour of their own; giving themselves and others Diversion with the mischief they make.

And it's ten to one but there's some old depending Servant, Nurse, or Neighbour, that thinks to ingratiate themselves into our Favour, by whispering in our ear after this manner.

Ah good Lady! the World does not go now as it did in our younger days: we were not wont to have it at this pass when I first knew you, nor need it be so now if things were well manag'd; but young Folks will not be advis'd; no body regards what we old Folk say. With many more such like Incentives.

But let us consider whether any thing of this kind be worth hearkening to. The World is still the same, and will be to the world's end, tho Modes and Manners alter yearly; most things are upon the Improvement: We see Arts and Sciences increase daily; Ornamental Ingenuity is more **[PP 13]** conspicuous in every degree: I see nothing that's wanting in general, but Truth and Honesty; and I heartily wish there were more that wou'd help cultivate these, in their own nature, universal Benefits. Yet *Solomon* bids us

(10)
not say of these times they are worse then the
former for thou doest not inquire wisely concerning
this.
You say things were never at this pass, But
were they in no case worse It is with some rea-
-son indeed that you think yr own method of man-
-agement best or else why did you choose to do it
in that manner. But you may consider yt times
& some few differing circumstances quite alter
the ~~nature~~ appearance of things, So that what was fitting
at one ^ time may be very preposterous at an-other
To have acted our own parts well affords a satis-
-factory reflection, we are very narrow in our
thoughts, if we conceit there is but one way of
well doing; Some can govern better with a nod,
then others with severities; Some heads can
spare their hands; And where they can't industry
may compensate for ingenuity, The Psalmist
tells us more emphatically then the Proverb, that
even rising early we may be in vain, so little 13
can we prescribe rules of our own.
Let us think how little we shou'd like to be
obliged to conform to ye modes of some few
ages past, what fault shou'd we find with
our Forefathers for what wou'd now appear
fantasticall; ~~were~~ is it not unreasonable to deny
any ~~one~~ the use of Tea, & Coffey, because their

not say of these Times, they are worse than the former; for thou dost not inquire wisely concerning this.

You say things were never at this pass: but were they in no case worse? It is with some reason indeed that you think your own Method of Management best, or else why did you chuse to do it in that manner? But you may consider that Times, and some few differing Circumstances, quite alter the appearance of things; so that what was fitting at one time, may be very preposterous at another. To have acted our own parts well affords a satisfactory Reflection: We are very narrow in our thoughts, if we conceit there is but one way of well-doing. Some can govern better with a Nod, than others with Severities: some Heads can spare their Hands; and where they can't, Industry may compensate for Ingenuity. The Psalmist tells us more emphatically than the Proverb, that even rising early, *&c.*[17] may be in vain; so little can we prescribe Rules of our own.[18]

[PP 14] Let us think how little we should like to be oblig'd to conform to the Modes of some few Ages past. What fault shou'd we find with our Forefathers, for what wou'd now appear fantastical? Is it not unreasonable to deny any the use of Tea and Coffee, because their

45 (41)

Mothers thought a toast & ale ye better breakfast;
In like women may not those that come after us esteem
what's most in vogue in their time best, as we
do now in ours If we are allow'd ye freedome to
choose for our Selves it is enough, we may as
freely let others do the like.
But perhaps you'l say here's such missmanage-
-ment as will bring whole families to ruine; If
it be through dissolute living, I grant that every
stone shou'd be turn'd to work a reformation;
yet here I think, the most ingaging Insinuations
shou'd first be tryed from ye affection we bear
to the Body, & Soul, of our Posterity, in whom
we hope to live many ages, For methinks those
Parents; who are honourably Succeeded by their
own Children, may be rather said to step out of
the way, then ever to Die.
In such Extremities it is so much our duty, & inter-
14 -est, to bring them to reason, that if fair means
faile, we ought certainly to use all the degrees of
rigor within our power to reclaim them if possible
For what fellowship hath righteousness with un-
righteousness, or Christ with Belial; to help
cultivate a good correspondence I am endeavouring
to reclame the lesser disorders, as the fitter task
for my small abilities
If young people are so imprudent as to live beyond
their income, it is Seasonable to remind them

Mothers thought a Toast and Ale the better Breakfast? In like manner, may not those that come after us esteem what's most in vogue in their time best, as we do now in ours? If we are allow'd the freedom to chuse for our selves, it is enough; we may as freely let others do the like.

But perhaps you'l say, Here's such Mismanagement as will bring whole Families to ruin. If it be thro dissolute Living, I grant that every Stone shou'd be turn'd to work a Reformation. Yet here, I think, the most ingaging Insinuations shou'd first be try'd, from the Affections we bear to the Body and Soul of our Posterity, in whom we hope to live many Ages. For methinks those Parents, who are honourably succeeded by their own Children, may be rather said to step out of the way, than ever to die.

In such Extremities, it is so much our Duty and Interest to bring them to Reason, that if fair means fail, we ought certainly to use all the degrees of Rigor within our power, to reclaim them if possible. *For* **[PP 15]** *what fellowship hath Righteousness with Unrightneousness, or Christ with Belial?*[19] To help cultivate a good Correspondence,[20] I am endeavouring to reclaim the lesser Disorders, as the fitter Task for my small Abilities.

If young People are so imprudent as to live beyond their Income, it is seasonable to remind them,

(12)

that if it be hard for them to live on what they have, it will be much harder to live on less then they now possess; And if they venture on ye expectation of a revertion, some Lucky hit, or the like, it's more then probable, they will thus be necessitous all their lives, He, that can fix no bounds, lies open to every expen-sive temptation, Whereas could they account of Revertions &c, only as of treasure lockt up in their Cabinets, ready to answer their latest occasions, then they would find the true benifit of them.

Let them spend no more then what's their own, & I would not much quarell at ye manner of it; if they like worse meat: with better sauce; or lay out more in china; then I did in plate; make two slight Sutes oftner then I did a good one, sure they may make their proportions agreeable to their own pleasure; it's most likely I steer'd by ye same rule: Besides tis to be considered that fancy differs as 15 much as faces.

Old people are very apt to conceipt themselves slighted without cause, & by talking much of it, they often put young:ones in mind to do it, it were better never to suppose any such thing, resting assured of your own goodwill towards all, with intentions to do benefits to all as occation offers, And every one has it in their power to be civil & obliging in behaviour, avoiding irksome complaints of any kind, which can little releeve the complainer & sours all conversation especially with the

That if it be hard for them to live on what they have, it will be much harder to live on less than they now possess; and if they venture on the expectation of a Reversion,[21] some lucky Hit, or the like, it's more than probable, they will thus be necessitous all their lives. He that can fix no bounds, lies open to every expensive Temptation: whereas could they account of Reversions, *&c.* only as of Treasure lock'd up in their Cabinets, ready to answer their latest Occasions;[22] then they would find the true benefit of them.

Let them spend no more than what's their own, and I would not much quarrel at the manner of it. If they like worse Meat with better Sauce; or lay out more in China, than I did in Plate; make two slight Sutes oftner than I did a good one:[23] sure they may make their Proportions agreeable to their own pleasure; it's most likely I steer'd by the same Rule. Besides, 'tis to be consider'd, that Fancy differs as much as Faces.

[PP 16] Old People are very apt to conceit[24] themselves slighted without cause; and by talking much of it, they often put young ones in mind to do it. It were better never to suppose any such thing, resting assur'd of your own Good-will towards all, with Intention to do benefits to all as occasion offers. And every one has it in their power to be civil and obliging in Behaviour, avoiding irksom Complaints of any kind, which can little relieve the Complainer, and sours all Conversation, especially with the

46 (25)

Yonger sort, who have yet tasted nothing of that
kind, & have no relish for it.
Therefore it were to be wish'd, we could in age most-
-ly chuse our conversation with those of sutable years,
who having known each other in their prime, con-
-sider them as then. But as this cannot always be
we must ye rather endeavour to fit our selves to our
company, As far as is consistent with Religion, &
the decency of that Character we bear. When pres-
-sed in either of these we ought to retire, fairly
supposing our company is not desired. And tis
but labour in vain to stem ye tide of loose talkers,
They are most happy who can say, I will go &
16 injoy my Self, by my Selfe.
As St Paul became all things to all Men to gain
Bpma 17. some, We may go far out of our own track to pre-
-serve that good-will, & affection, which we may at
other times make use of to much better purposes.
Thus we may very Innocently use severall games
to oblige others, & divert our selves, so we do not
shew too much fondness for them, nor make them
an occation of any passion or disorder. Children
reckon a little mony thus got of Parents very Sweet
And I reckon it very well bestow'd tho it keep them
only from bad company, wch they might otherwise
seek for their diversion. It will turn to better ac-
-count then to leave them hoards when we die &

younger sort, who have yet tasted nothing of that kind, and have no relish for it.[25]

Therefore it were to be wish'd, we could in Age mostly chuse our conversation with those of sutable Years, who having known each other in their prime, consider them as then. But as this cannot always be, we must the rather endeavour to fit our selves to our Company, as far as is consistent with Religion, and the Decency of that Character we bear. When press'd in either of these, we ought to retire; fairly supposing our Company is not desir'd. And 'tis but labour in vain to stem the Tide of loose Talkers: They are most happy who can say, I will go and enjoy my self, by my self.

As St. *Paul* became all things to all Men, to gain some,[26] we may go far out of our own **[PP 17]** track to preserve that Good-will and Affection, which we may at other times make use of to much better purposes. Thus we may very innocently use several Games to oblige others, and divert our selves; so we do not shew too much fondness for them, nor make them an occasion of any Passion of Disorder. Children reckon a little Mony thus got of Parents very sweet. And I reckon it very well bestow'd, tho it keep them only from bad Company; which they might otherwise seek for their diversion. It will turn to better account than to leave them Hoards when we die, and

(14)

can no longer keep it. If we are doubtfull of their misspending mony, I have thought it a prety way that all winnings be laid by in bank for a sum. to purchase some usefull thing at their own Election. If we desire to live easy a-bove all things let us be-ware of Jealousy of every kind, for as soon as that takes place, we conclude the worst, yet add the perplexity of much search, & many inventions to confirm it to ourselves. When perhaps halfe that painfull contrivance might remove the occation, or fortifie us to bear ye worst we fear. For suppose it were even the distrust that a husband does not regard our company, or prefers some other before us. First let us reflect on our own demerit. and regulate what's in our power by a sincere amend-ment; let us learn by what arts others engaged him; but not frowardly ubraid him; if he's not a brute Good humour supported with virtue may offer many Insinuations to help us keep Possession; If we can overcome our own resentment, ye Conquest is near gain'd; For the teazing part, wch blows ye coals is removed from either side. And that we may the more easily overcome ourselves we shou'd by no means suffer any body else to feed us with any thing of that nature. Thus may it be in things of lesser concernment; Perhaps we suspect our Lives are not desired, Or yt some sport themselves with our can no longer keep 'em. If we are doubtful of their mispending Mony, I have thought it a pretty way that all Winnings[27] be laid by in bank for a Sum, to purchase some useful thing at their own election.

If we desire to live easy, above all things let us beware of Jealousy of every kind; for as soon as that takes place, we conclude the worst, yet add the perplexity of much Search, and many Inventions to confirm it to our selves: when perhaps half that painful Contrivance might remove the Occasion, or fortify us to bear the worst we fear. For suppose it were even the Distrust that a Husband does not regard our Company, or prefers some other before us: First, Let us reflect on our own **[B]** [**PP 18**] Demerit, and regulate what's in our power by a sincere Amendment: Let us learn by what Arts others engag'd him; but not frowardly upbraid him. If he's not a Brute, Good Humour supported with Virtue may offer many Insinuations to help us keep possession. If we can overcome our own Resentment, the Conquest is near gain'd; for the teazing part, which blows the Coal,[28] is remov'd from either side. And that we may the more easily overcome our selves, we shou'd by no means suffer any body else to feed us with any thing of that nature. Thus may it be in things of lesser concernment: Perhaps we suspect our Lives are not desir'd, or that some sport themselves with our

47 (15)

Infirmities & the like. Never let us reprove such
faults directly, least they cast it as a saving to our
selves, rather shew them the ill manners of it towards
others We shou'd do well to manifest ourselves not
unwilling to die, whenever it shall please God to
call us; It is best to think much, & yet to talk little
of dying least it be reply'd after ye manner One is
said to do to his Wife, Prethy talk no more of this
dismall hour, but set yr time & stand to it.

It argues great indiscretion in any one to sport
2 themselves with ye infirmities of their Parents,
from whose stock they derive their own Being & so
are likely to participate: mockery was severly re-
-prov'd by Gods Judgment on ye rude children who
only cry'd; go up thou bald pate, there are scarse
any, who wish to die young to avoid the infirmities
of Age, And as ther's no perfection in humane
Nature, we may be (nay all are) liable to the re-
-proach of carping criticks.

If it be evident that our company is shunn'd, let us
consider whence it proceeds, If from a sowr conver-
-sation & a thwarting temper, we have it in
our power to find a remedy, if it be from a strict
virtue, wch will countenance nothing vitious
or prophane; let us be thankfull to God, that he
has given us such a distinguishing Qualificati-
-on, which will enable us to take more pleasure
in Heavenly conversation, & make us less value

Infirmities, and the like. Never let us reprove such Faults directly, lest they construe it as a Saving to our selves; but rather shew them the Ill-manners of it towards others.

We shou'd do well to manifest our selves not unwilling to die, whenever it shall please God to call us. It is best to think much, and yet to talk little of dying, lest it be reply'd after the manner one is said to have done to his Wife: *Prithee, talk no more of this dismal Hour; but set your time, and stand to it.*
[pp 19] It argues great Indiscretion in any one, to Sport themselves with the Infirmities of their Parents, from whose Stock they derive their own Being, and so are likely to participate. Mockery was severely reprov'd by God's judgment on the rude Children, who only cry'd, *Go up, thou Bald-pate!*[29] There are scarce any who wish to die young to avoid the Infirmities of Age: And as there's no Perfection in human Nature, we may be (nay all are) liable to the Reproach of carping Criticks.

If it be evident that our Company is shun'd, let us consider when it proceeds. If from a sour Conversation and a thwarting Temper, we have it in our power to find a Remedy: if it be from a strict Virtue, which will countenance nothing vicious or profane; let us be thankful to God, that he has given us such a distinguishing Qualification, which will enable us to take more pleasure in Heavenly Conversation, and make us less value

(16)
worldly Enjoyments. Old people are commonly
allow'd a decent retirement, & we shou'd do well to be
so provided, that it may not be irksome to us to
be alone; This may be acquir'd by some times
using to withdraw when we might have compa-
-ny, entertaining our selves with Bookes, ye Pen,
& such little works, as sute with age which we
should be provided for before it comes — for
it's then very difficult to learn any new thing; 3
In all Ages a full imployment is of singular use
especially to such tempers as are trouble'd with
foreboding thoughts, & evil surmises.
Are any Angry for their not being admitted into
the secrets of the family; Even this is their pri-
viledge that they are not burthen'd with a secret;
And as they were not consulted, they are not now
answerable for any misscarriages & avoid all sus-
-picion of having disclosed the matter.
But say it looks unkind, that common things shou'd be conceal'd
if it be so, have not ye freedoms
of conversation been some way misused; either by
disaproving what others say, right or wrong, & thence
occation taken to thwart their purposes, Exer-
-cising a supposed Authority, which in this case
amounts to no more then to shew one has it in
ones Power to make Discord; Or has it not been
made a subject of discourse to others with

worldly Enjoyments. Old People are commonly allow'd a decent Retirement; and we shou'd do well to be so provided, that it may not be irksom to us to be alone. This may be acquir'd by sometimes using to withdraw when we might have Company, entertaining our selves with Books, the Pen, and such little Works, as **[B2][PP 20]** sute with Age, which we should be provided for before it comes: for it's then very difficult to learn any new thing. In all Ages a full Employment is of singular use, especially to such Tempers as are troubled with foreboding Thoughts, and evil Surmises.

Are any angry for their not being admitted into the Secrets of the Family? Even this is their Privilege, that they are not burden'd with a Secret; and as they were not consulted, they are not now answerable for any Miscarriages, and avoid all Suspicion of having disclos'd the matter.

But say it looks unkind, that common things should be conceal'd: Be it so. Have not the Freedoms of Conversation been some way misus'd? either by disapproving what others say, right or wrong; and thence occasion taken to thwart their purposes, exercising a suppos'd Authority, which in this case amounts to no more than the shew one has it in one's power to make Discord. Or has it not been made a Subject of Discourse to others, with

118 (28)

Reflections thereon perhaps to ye disadvantage of partyes concern'd.

If without these or such like causes, there be an un-decent shyness in conversation, let us Indeavour to off by letting others see how safely they may repose any trust in us, & what regard we have to their satisfaction.

4 If there be Man & Wife at ye head of ye family we shou'd do our utmost to cherish a good understanding betwixt them to preserve ye peace of the whole. For if they have any seperate Intrests, Designs, or but Corresspondents, that are disagreeable to each other, it will be very dificult to maintain the goodwill of both. Therefore we shou'd not appear to side with either, but in private perswade both to those things wch are most reasonable, & may bring ym nearest to Agreement Always remembering, that if it be not in a matter sinfull, condescention is the Womans Duty: There is hardly any cause, that can tolerate her being clamorous with a husband; If she cannot mildly bring him to reason, She must content her Self under the shelter of her Obedience.

Matters of expence is the most common cause of these differences, It's therfore best calmly to consider this point between themselves & make proportions accord-ing to their circumstances, & each knowing their part must be truly iust & free with ye other the wo-man not ashamed to produce her particular account

Reflections thereon, perhaps to the disadvantage of the Parties concern'd?

If without these, or such-like Causes, there be an undecent Shyness in Conversation; let us endeavour to wipe it off, by letting others see how safely they may **[PP 21]** repose any Trust in us, and what regard we have to their satisfaction.

If there be Man and Wife at the Head of the Family, we shou'd do our utmost to cherish a good Understanding betwixt them, to preserve the Peace of the whole. For if they have any separate Interests, Designs, or but Correspondents, that are disagreeable to each other, it will be very difficult to maintain the Good-will of both. Therefore we shou'd not appear to side with either, but in private persuade both to those things which are most reasonable, and may bring them nearest to Agreement: always remembring, that if it be not in a matter sinful, Condescension is the Woman's Duty. There is hardly any Cause, that can tolerate her being clamorous with a Husband. If she cannot mildly bring him to Reason, she must content her self under the shelter of her Obedience.

Matters of Expence is the most common Cause of these Differences: It's therefore best, calmly to consider this Point between themselves, and make proportions according to their Circumstances; and each knowing their part, must be truly just and free with the other: the Woman not asham'd to produce her particular Account

(18)

of disburtsments, For it's more commendable to spend what we lay out well; then that much shoud run through our hands; And having food & raiment let us be therewith content; That is with such a degree of it, as we can fairly, & freely attain; Such exceedings as must be labour'd for in any clandestine way, can never afford answerable Satisfaction in the end, tho at present they may please with their gaudy shew; If we cant restrain a desire after fine things, nay & for some sorts of conveniencyes too, there will be no bounds to our cravings & thus we are like always to live in want; They only are Rich, who think they have enough, & find something to spare upon any Emergency.

The woman gives up her title & can make no seperate demand after marriage; Surely therfore it will be her Interest to convince her Husband, that she desires to spend no more then what may handsomly throughout every part carry on the decency of that rank they hold in the world with a due consideration for the main-chance; Tis now too late to expostulate, or stand on terms proportionable, it may be, to what she brought the Stock is United, & become but One; the Husband has an unquestionable Command over that, as well as her Person.

If by compliance & some little observances we can gain the Goodwill of those, that have the ascendant over us; it's an easy way to make our selves happy; For when once we secure their good opinion, they must be ill tured to deny us the liberty of our own choice of Disbursements. For it's more commendable to spend **[B3][PP 22]** what we lay out well, than that much shou'd run thro our hands: and having Food and Raiment,[30] let us be therewith content; that is, with such a degree of it, as we can fairly and freely attain. Such Exceedings as must be labour'd for in any clandestine way, can never afford answerable Satisfaction in the end, tho at present they may please with their gaudy shew. If we can't restrain a Desire after fine things, nay and for some sort of Conveniences too, there will be no bounds to our Cravings; and thus we are like always to live in want. They only are rich, who think they have enough, and find something to spare upon any Emergency.

The Woman gives up her Title, and can make no separate Demand after Marriage. Surely therefore it will be her Interest to convince her Husband, that she desires to spend no more than what may handsomly throughout every part carry on the Decency of that Rank they hold in the World, with a due Consideration for the main Chance.[31] 'Tis now too late to expostulate, or stand on terms proportionable, it may be, to what she brought: the Stock is united, and become but one; the Husband has an unquestionable Command over that, as well as her Person.

[PP 23] If by Compliance, and some little Observances, we can gain the Good-will of those that have the ascendent over us; it's an easy way to make our selves happy. For when once we secure their good Opinion, they must be ill-natur'd to deny us the liberty of our own Choice

49 (19)

in things indifferent. & the mere materiall one would
choose to submit to them; it being by much the easier
6 task to obey, then to command well: But to return
from this digression: For those, who are retired from com
-mand leaving the Stage to others, are the chief Subjects
of these transients thoughts.
As often as any Child or Grandchild is prefer'd before others
in the same relation, such Partiality will give occation
for the murmurs of the rest. I deny not that some distinc
-tion may be made according to their good Qualities,
but then it must plainly appear, that this is the ground
they go upon, by setting each virtue, wherever placed
find it's suitable Incouragement.
If any plead that affections are not so much in our
own power as that we can truly help the loving one
~~person~~ better then an other, tho we have no obligation
so to do; for when we happen into the company of
meer Strangers, we shall find a much stronger in-
-clination towards some then to others at first sight,
it may well be question'd whither this is not often
a delusive Affection: Granting we cannot help some
Partiality in love, Discretion may nevertheless so
govern that affection, as in a manner to keep it a
secret to our Selves, by making so little difference
in the publick marks of kindness: That the rest
may have no reason to complain, nor standers by
see any cause for Jealousy, wch is often raised
by others observation where this falls in with a

in things indifferent; and the more material one wou'd chuse to submit to them, it being by much the easier task to obey, than to command, well. But to return from this Digression: For those, who are retir'd from Command, leaving the Stage to others, are the chief Subjects of these transient Thoughts.

As often as any Child or Grandchild is prefer'd before others in the same Relation, such Partiality will give occasion for the murmur of the rest. I deny not that some distinction may be made according to their good Qualities; but then it must plainly appear, that this is the ground they go upon, by letting each Virtue, wherever plac'd, finds its sutable Encouragement.

If any plead that Affections are not so much in our own power, as that we can truly help the loving one better than another, tho we have no Obligation so to do; for when we happen into the Company of mere Strangers, we shall find a much stronger Inclination towards some than to others at first **[B4][PP 24]** sight: it may well be question'd whether this is not often a delusive Affection. Granting we cannot help some Partiality in Love, Discretion may nevertheless so govern that Affection, as in a manner to keep the Secret to our selves, by making so little difference in the publick Marks of Kindness, that the rest may have no reason to complain, nor Standers by see any cause for Jealousy; which is often rais'd by others Observation, where this falls in with a

(20)

suspicious temper.
I know people are apt to be blindly carryed on 7
with a fond passion without discerning by what
means it grows & overcomes them; A Child with
a fawning insinuation is liable to do a world of
mischief, if not carefully observed: It's first pre-
-ty talk we admire & commend, which ye child
soon finds; both parties are pleased & incourag-
-ed to go on; By gradual steps ye child gets full
possestion of the ear; the only care then is to ga-
-ther matter enough to entertain it; And the
fertile brain will call over all the transactions of
the family & of every individual person in it,
& perhaps go as far into the neighbourhood as
their knowledg reaches; it is well if by this time
it do's not go beyond it's knowledg & tell more
then it has either heard or seen: for nature
prompts them to inlarge these pleasing confer
rences: Now tho it may delight [illegible] to hear
things thus related by the Beloved Innocent.
yet when we come to chew over all this crude
stuff, we must needs find a great deal that
we can neither relish, nor digest; yet we must
keep it in least by uttering it, we stop the
sourse, which supplies this craving appetite;
And do we think this can breed good bloud, or 8
turn to any better account, then ye sowing

suspicious Temper.

I know People are apt to be blindly carry'd on with a fond Passion, without discerning by what means it grows and overcomes them. A Child with a fawning Insinuation is liable to do a world of mischief, if not carefully observ'd. Its first pretty Talk we admire and commend, which the Child soon finds: both Parties are pleas'd, and encourag'd to go on. By gradual steps the Child gets full possession of the Ear: the only Care then is to gather matter enough to entertain it; and the fertile Brain will call over all the Transactions of the Family, and of every individual Person in it, and perhaps go as far into the Neighbourhood as their Knowledge reaches. It is well if by this time it does not go beyond its Knowledg, and tell more than it has either **[PP 25]** heard or seen; for Nature prompts them to enlarge these pleasing Conferences. Now tho it may delight to hear things thus related by the beloved Innocent, yet when we come to chew over all this crude Stuff, we must needs find a great deal that we can neither relish nor digest; yet we must keep it in, lest by uttering it, we stop the Source. which supplies this craving Appetite. And do we think this can breed good Blood, or turn to any better account, than the sowing

30 (21)

of many evil seeds, some of wch will undoubtedly
take root. the disquiet of the whole family is
almost inevitable where one private favorite is
set up to engross what others might equally
clame.

Therefore if we see some excellencies prefer-
-able in one, we shou'd also see their defects, &
search for good properties in the Rest; Providence
usually throws something solid into that scale, wch
appears to be over borne; most have something Good;
none are Perfect; let us examine well whether
those, who most carress us, do not more seek their
own satisfaction, then ours; And let this considerati-
-on extend not only to Children, but unto all, who
wou'd fawn us into a good opinion of themselves to
the prejudice of others, Thus, tis plain, we had need
guard our ears even from those, that speak us fair;
for soft words may prove such a murmering wind
as sometimes blows up a very small spark into a
consuming fire, where it happens to light on com-
-bustable matter in a breast dispos'd to take fire.

There is an other failing I can't over look, tho it
seems of little moment And tis the general com-
-plaint, among old people especially, of the badness of
9 servants, The cry often runs: that if servants were
-not so strangely perverse & mischeivious, but would
do their proper parts, they cou'd be easy & do well
enough. I wish in earnest there were less ground

of many evil Seeds, some of which will undoubtedly take root? The Disquiet of the whole Family is almost inevitable, where one private Favorite is set up, to engross what others might equally claim.

Therefore if we see some Excellencies preferable in one, we shou'd also see their Defects, and search for good Properties in the rest. Providence usually throws something solid into the Scale, which appears to be overborn: most have something good; none are perfect. Let us examine well, whether those who most caress us, do not more seek their own Satisfaction, than ours. And let this Consideration extend not only to Children, but unto all, who wou'd fawn us into a good Opinion of themselves, to the prejudice of others. Thus, 'tis plain, we had need guard our Ears, even from those, **[PP 26]** that speak us fair: for soft words may prove such a murmuring Wind, as sometimes blows up a very small Spark into a consuming Fire, where it happens to light on combustible Matter, in a Breast dispos'd to take fire.

There is another Failing I can't overlook, tho it seems of little moment; and 'tis the general Complaint, among old People especially, of the Badness of Servants. The Cry often runs, That if Servants were not so strangley perverse and mischievous, but would do their proper parts, they cou'd be easy, and do well enough. I wish in earnest there were less ground

[22]

for this complaint; there needs more then common
prudence to regulate the overgrown height of servants:
Those Mistresses are deservedly blam'd, who have incou-
-raged their pride, falsely thinking their finery
gives some reputation to their place & themselves;
whereas this do's but excite their pride wch is ye
root of all vanity, destroying industry, sloth follows
& they soon forgat the Respect thats due to their
Superiors. yet let us see how much complaining
redresses this greivance & carry it no farther;
It's true we must sometimes chide & tell servants
their faults, or they wou'd never know they did amiss;
for we are not to expect so much ingenuity as that
they shou'd correct themselves. But then let us
do it in such a manner as may convince them of
the fault, makeing them see how they might have
done better: this may work something towards pre-
-venting the like an other time, whereas if we only
give them hard words with vehement anger, dwell-
ing long upon it, we are more likely to raise their savage
passion, which will farther provoke, or perhaps they will
fling away sullenly, pleasing themselves with some sort
of revenge by carrying the crime still higher. The best 10
we can expect from loud clamour is to make them
fear our thunder, wch to a timerous mind may occation
more faults, if we have such to deal with; overawing
ym will make fear predominate & prevent free
thinking, which shou'd help contrive every thing to

for this Complaint. There needs more than common Prudence to regulate the overgrown Height of Servants. Those Mistresses are deservedly blam'd, who have encourag'd their Pride, falsly thinking their Finery gives some Reputation to their Place and themselves: whereas this does but excite their Pride, which is the Root of all Vanity, destroying Industry; Sloth follows, and they soon forget the Respect that's due to their Superiors. Yet let us consider how much complaining redresses this Grievance, and carry it no farther. It's true, we must sometimes chide and tell Servants their Faults, or they wou'd never know they did amiss: for we are not to expect so much Ingenuity, as that they shou'd correct themselves. But **[PP 27]** then let us do it in such a manner as may convince them of the Fault, making them see how they might have done better. This may work something towards preventing the like another time: whereas if we only give them hard words with vehement Anger, dwelling long upon it, we are more likely to raise their savage Passion; which will farther provoke, or perhaps they will fling away sullenly, pleasing themselves with some sort of Revenge, by carrying the Crime still higher. The best we can expect from loud Clamour, is to make them fear our Thunder, which to a timorous Mind may occasion more Faults, if we have such to deal with: overawing them will make Fear predominate, and prevent free Thinking, which shou'd help contrive every thing to

51 (23)

the best advantage: violent anger shou'd only
oppose violent faults; we must distinguish meer
accidents & inadvertencies, from an evil dispositi
& contrived mischief; the former deserve some pity
and our care to help their failings; the latter (as ye
root lies deep) can hardly be cured but by a
thorough conviction in themselves; Yet severity
may restrain them, & is most properly [illegible] to such,
perhaps hard service, with little liberty, may work
more upon them then many words; it's a common
saying, that they, who chide for every fault, will
have none mended; we must sometimes looke
through our fingers, that is see, & not see, try first
to mend ye greater faults & many lesser one's will
drop off with them; It may not be a-miss to sup-
-pose our selves in our servants steads & consider,
whither, under their circumstances, we could com
-ply with all those capricious humors, they have
11 to deal withall: If once servants take ye conceipt
that, by chiding, we gratifie our own peivish
humour, they will no longer regard what we say;
but only endeavour to harden themselves against it,
or make it a matter of diversion among their own
consorts;
If no means will take effect to reclaim &
make servants usefull to us; we have yet this

the best advantage. Violent Anger shou'd only oppose violent Faults. We must distinguish mere Accidents and Inadvertencies, from an evil Disposition and contriv'd Mischief: the former deserve some Pity, and our Care to help their Failings; the latter (as the Root lies deep) can hardly be cur'd but by a thorow[32] Conviction in themselves: yet Severity may restrain them, and is most properly apply'd to such; perhaps hard Service, with little Liberty, may work more upon them than many words. It's a com-**[PP 28]** mon Saying, That they who chide for every Fault, will have none mended. We must sometimes look thro our fingers, that is, see and not see; try first to mend the greater Faults, and many lesser ones will drop off with them. It may not be amiss to suppose our selves in our Servants stead, and consider whether, under their Circumstances, we could comply with all those capricious Humours they have to deal withal. If once Servants take the conceit,[33] that by chiding we gratify our own peevish Humour, they will no longer regard what we say, but only endeavour to harden themselves against it, or make it a matter of Diversion among their own Consorts.[34]

If no means will take effect to reclaim and make Servants useful to us, we have yet this

(24)

remidy to put them from us when their time is out; And it's not reasonable to complain much of those evils we see through; But if we think to find servants, that shall sute & please us in every thing, we must still be disappoynted; we can hardly please our selves at all times, nor can those, who are nearest to us by affinity, in interest, or by obligation, always hit each others fancy, or do whats best pleasing to them, although they aime at it. And surely we are much less to expect it from servants. If they obey our commands according to ye best of their skill, we need not be outrageous at their other faults, experience with practice will increase every day where there is a capacity for it, If indeed that be wanting, those are most to blame who put them upon undertaking such business as nature never designed them for 12

I do not approve the being familiar with servants in their sports, & foolish jestings, but a serious familiarity in business, & the needfull transactions of life is what may be profitable on all sides, & will heighten rather then lessen their respects to such Superiors.

If we complain of all servants alike, makeing no difference, or like none, at least till they are gone from us, perhaps to some better place, It is shrewdly

Remedy, to put them from us when their Time is out. And it's not reasonable to complain much of those Evils we see thro. But if we think to find Servants that shall sute and please us in every thing, we must still be disappointed; we can hardly please our selves at all times, nor can those who are nearest to us by Affinity, in Interest, or by Obligation, always hit each others Fancy, or do what's best pleasing to them, altho they aim at it. And surely we are much less to expect it from Servants. If they **[PP 29]** obey our Commands according to the best of their skills, we need not be outrageous at their other Faults. Experience with Practice will increase every day, where there is a Capacity for it: If indeed that be wanting, those are most to blame who put them upon undertaking such Business as Nature ne'er design'd them for.

I do not approve the being familiar with Servants in their Sports, and foolish Jestings; but a serious Familiarity in Business, and the needful Transactions of Life, is what may be profitable on all sides, and will heighten rather than lessen their Respects to such Superiors.

If we complain of all Servants alike, making no difference; or like none, at least till they are gone from us, perhaps to some better Place; it is shrewdly

52 (25)

suspicious that we have an uneasy temper, & think
to preserve our selves from ye imputation by giving
the most decent vent. to this sharp humour, which
puts me in mind of the Divine Herberts advice

Be kind to all, 'tis y^r complection sowre
Keep such company, make y^m your Allay,
Get a sharp wife, or servans, y^t will sowre:
A stumbler stumbles least in rugged Way.

B 14. Surely did we but observe the deformity of ill na-
-tured anger in others; it would much help to work
the cure in our selves.
I have hitherto been perswading Ancient people to
exert their utmost power in shewing good humour
towards others Now to keep the Elder women in
good humour with themselves also, I will give ~~them~~
13 some instances wherein they are generally Esteem'd
Benefits & usefull in their Generation.
Q. 1. M. A Teeming woman can have no better incouragment
for assistance then from such an experienced friend
at time of need. And young Children can hardly be
brought up without the advice & directions of those,
who have before had the like care. These tender fibers
are soon disordered through inadvertency; numerous
small ailments attend them, wch an unwary eye
observes not till a worse consequence follows, and a
common remedy might at first have rectified; even
Celebrated Nurses will often overlook many symptoms,

suspicious that we have an uneasy Temper, and think to preserve our selves from the Imputation,[35] by giving the most decent Vent to this sharp Humour. Which puts me in mind of the Divine *Herbert's* Advice:[36]

Be kind to all: Is your Complection sour?
Keep such Company, make them your Allay;[37]
Get a Sharp Wife, or Servant, that will lour:[38]
A Stumbler stumbles least in rugged Way.

[PP 30] Surely did we but observe the deformity of ill-natur'd Anger in others, it wou'd much help to work the Cure in our Selves.

I have hitherto been persuading antient[39] People to exert their utmost Power in shewing good Humour towards others. Now to keep the elder Woman in good Humour with themselves also, I will give some Instances wherein they are generally esteem'd Benefits, and useful in their Generation.

A teeming[40] Woman can have not better Incouragement nor Assistance than from such an experience'd Friend at time of need. And young Children can hardly be brought up without the Advice and Directions of those, who have before had the like Care. These tender Fibres are soon disorder'd thro Inadvertency:[41] numerous small Ailments attend them, which an unwary Eye observes not till a worse consequence follows, and a common remedy might at first have rectified. Even celebrated Nurses will often overlook many Symptoms,

(26)

which an Affectionate bystander may discover, &
find a suteable remedy for, from their own experience:
Docters with children doe commonly only make tin-
-kering work instead of mending one fault they often
make more: When ye first distemper with its cause
is not apparent in an infant, that can't descrive the
pain, guesses are very uncertain, & strong medicins
are dangerous, so that it's much safer to depend on
nature, with only the help of some gentle remidies.

I am not perswading every body to qualifie them-
-selves for Midwifes & Nurses, Yet think no
degree of Quality excuses such an Ignorance as
that when advanc'd in years they should not be
able from their own observations to give some
seasonable advice, & directions in common cases, 14
for, all ranks stand in ye same degree of concern for
their own family, & friends. And none can always
be sure of having such assistanse at hand as they
may chance to need Some Ingenuous Nobility
have complained, that they were hardly ever taught
the use of their hands, so that they do but aukward
-ly know how to tie a knot, or stick a pin; but in
lesser quality we can scarse impute it to Ignorance,
that many are so backward in affording any assistance
at time of need, I rather fear some niceties withhold
them: Disdainfull ladyes may stop their ears to a
crying child, & never listen to any groans, nor once
venture to peep into a sick chamber, Yet they cannot

which an affectionate By-Stander may discover, and find a sutable remedy for, from their own Experience: Doctors with Children too commonly only make tinkering Work; instead of mending one fault, they often make more. When the first Distemper with its Cause is not apparent in an Infant, that can't describe the **[PP 31]** Pain, Guesses are very uncertain, and strong Medicines are dangerous; so that it's much safer to depend on Nature, with only the help of some gentle Remedys.

I am not persuading every body to qualify themselves for Midwives and Nurses. Yet think no degree of Quality excuses such an Ignorance, as that when advanc'd in years they shou'd not be able, from their own Observations, to give some seasonable Advice, and Directions in common Cases: for all Ranks stand in the same degree of concern for their own Family and Friends; and none can always be sure of having such Assistance at hand as they may chance to need. Some ingenuous Nobility have complain'd, that they were hardly ever taught the use of their hands; so that they do but aukwardly know how to tie a Knot, or stick a Pin: but in lesser Quality we can scarce impute it to Ignorance, that many are so backward in affording any Assistance at time of need; I rather fear some Niceties withhold them. Disdainful Ladys may stop their Ears to a crying Child, and never listen to any Groans, nor once venture to peep into a sick Chamber; yet they cannot

53 (27)

secure themselves from the like Calamities; And who is there, that under Pain, Sickness, & Distress, does-not think it a mighty comfort to have a serious friend near them, who with tenderness will hearken to all their complaints, condole their grief, studying how to releive them with all the assistance their condition admits. cheerfully incouraging their Patience to help support the tottering frame when such a friend may perhaps also be assisting to preserve the order of ye family. which their owne present indisposition will not allow them to take care of: I need not inlarge on this Benefitt beleiveing every one's experience must give them a true sense of it

14 It may sometimes very much oblige young House-keepers, if we offer to take upon us the care of their families. for a while; in their Lyings-in, or to give them ye better opportunity of going abroad, or takeing a Journey, or ye like. And by this trouble-some variety we shall gain a more pleasing relish for retirement; And I wou'd have this made the more a trouble by not persuing our own method of Go-vernment, but carrying it on in the best manner we can as dictated unto, or directed.

I plead for strict conformity to family government. as conducing much to ye happyness of life. If the younger live under the Elder they have the utmost reason to comply with such rules as their betters think fit, affording ym what help they can to lighten their burthen. And if the younger ones set at ye Helm secure themselves from the like Calamitys: and who is there, that under Pain, Sickness, and Distress, does not think it a mighty Comfort to have a serious Friend near them, who with tenderness will **[PP 32]** hearken to all their Complaints, condole their Grief, studying how to relieve them withall the Assistance their Condition admits, chearfully incouraging their Patience, to help support the tottering Frame? when such a Friend may perhaps also be assisting to preserve the Order of the Family, which their own present Indisposition will not allow them to take care of. I need not inlarge on this Benefit, believing every one's experience must give them a true sense of it.

It may sometimes very much oblige young Housekeepers, if we offer to take upon us the care of their Families for a while, in their Lyings-in, or to give them the better Opportunity of going abroad, and taking a Journy, or the like. And by this troublesom variety we shall gain a more pleasing relish of Retirement. And I would have this made the more a Trouble, by the not pursuing our own method of Government, but carrying things on in the best manner we can, as dictated unto, or directed.

I plead for strict Conformity to Family-Government, as conducting much to the Happiness of Life. If the Younger live under the Elder, they have the utmost reason to comply with such Rules as their Betters think fit, affording them what help they can to tighten their Burden. And if the younger Ones sit at the Helm,

(28)

the government is put into their hands, & for orders -sake must be maintained, the elder then have no more to do, But to advise, assist, & encourage them all they are able. Cpm 33

I have already recommended ye moderate use of some innocent divertions for ye entertainment of younger people.

The catechising & teaching instructing, of childeren, is a work of absolute neccity for their future well being, & most commonly 'tis ye Elders of ye family, that have the most leasure, & are ~~fittest~~ adapted to this usefull exercise; that fondness, wch in age we shew towards young ones, enables us to bear with their impertinencies, & furnishes us with means to ingratiate our-selves with them; I am now endeavouring in some respects to accomodate our selves to all degrees, therefore may here suggest, that old Women are always supposed to be furnished with pleaseing tales for childeren; ~~&~~ wch if well chosen may afford them both delight, & profit. 16

If our memorys serve, all the lovers of Hystory & Chronoligy will be delighted with a handsome relation of ye most remarkable transactions of our times. And here we have a fair occation for makeing proper reflections on the false measures, many mistaken politicks, & miss carrages, of Mankind. The rise & fall of many families The vicissitude of Fortune, And uncertainty of all Humane Affairs.

the Government is **[PP 33]** put into their hands, and for Order-sake must be maintain'd; the Elder then have no more to do, but to advise, assist, and encourage them all they are able.

I have already recommended the moderate use of some innocent Diversions for the entertainment of younger People.

The catechizing, instructing and teaching of Children, is a Work of absolute necessity for their future well-being; and most commonly 'tis the Elders of the Family, that have the most leisure, and are best adapted to this useful Exercise: that Fondness, which in Age we shew towards young Ones, enables us to bear with their Impertinencies, and furnishes us with means to ingratiate our selves with them. I am now endeavouring in some respects to accommodate our selves to all degrees; therefore may here suggest, that old Women are always suppos'd to be furnish'd with pleasing Tales for Children; which if well chosen, may afford them both Delight and Profit.

If our Memorys serve, all the Lovers of History and Chronology will be delighted with a hansom relation of the most remarkable Transactions of our Times. And here we have a fair occasion for making proper Reflections on the false measures, many mistaken Politicks, and Miscarriages of Man kind, the Rise and Fall of many Familys, the [C]**[PP 34]** Vicissitude of Fortune,[42] and Uncertainty of all Human Affairs:

51 (29)

The heedfull observation of such things: may be instruc-tive to succeeding ages.
To take in ye more, I will not omit; that even the young modemongers are pleased with some account of the fashions of former times, if we'l suffer ym to rediculе them as fantastick; And not inveigh against the present admir'd Dress, Or Address.

The most generall & Ingaging Vertue that we can practice is an extensive Charity in it's pro-per sense; 1 Cor: 13. For I do not mean a profuse squandring of mony to the detriment of our selves & those, who have a just clame to it; And it may many times be more charity to shut our hands, then to open them, to a Prodigal; It is ye doing of real Benefits (tho by Correction where needfull) that is acceptable to God, & profits all good people in the end.
If we have had opportunity to attain any com-petent skill in Phisick, or Surgery this will be a usefull charity that will gain us Esteem from the whole neighbourhood; in many places there's no learned advisers to be had; & if there be any such poor people, who can but just support their neces-sitys, are not able to bear this extrordinary charge If it be but a friendly visit to the distressed it often affords them a comfortable refreshment; And a word in season how good it is; our thoughts,

The heedful Observation of such things may be instructive to succeeding Ages.

To take in the more, I will not omit, that even the young Mode-mongers are pleas'd with some account of the Fashions of former times, if we'l suffer them to ridicule them as fantastick; and not inveigh against the present admir'd Dress, or Address.

The most general and ingaging Virtue that we can practise, is an extensive Charity in its proper sense, *I Cor:13*. For I do not mean a profuse squandring of Mony, to the detriment of our selves; and those who have a just Claim to it; and it may many times be more Charity to shut our Hands, than to open them to a Prodigal: It is the doing of real Benefits (tho by Correction where needful) that is acceptable to God, and profits all good People in the end.

If we have had opportunity to attain any competent Skill in Physick, or Surgery, this will be a useful Charity, that will gain us Esteem from the whole Neighbourhood. In many Places there's no learned Advisers to be had: and if there be any such, poor People, who can but just support their Necessitys, are not able to bear this extraordinary Charge. If it be but a friendly Visit to the Distress'd, it often affords them a [PP 35] comfortable Refreshment; and a work in season how good is it! Our Thoughts,

(30)

which are free from ye Depression of their trouble
may by an active search find out ye most proper
means for their releif.
To those Poor, who have health & strength; there is
no charity so Benificial as the keeping them in
constant imployment: For if we once bestow any
such gifts on them as will incourage their Pride 2
& sloth, we destroy Industry; labour will then
be irksome to them, and ruine must follow;
Whereas if youth are betimes enured to take
some pains in a busey life, it will be even bur-
densome for them to be Idle; They should always
be perswaded to think neatness a more becoming
finery, then gaudy lace, & ribons, And what
cloathing we bestow on them shou'd be fitted
more to their necessitys, then fancy
The putting young Children to school is a charity,
that, God be Praised, has prevailed very much
of late, & will, I hope, turn to a good account; if
not abused by too much Pedantry in the Teachers.
As the most Profligate wretches have always
charged themselves with the Profanation of the
Lords day, as that, wch has led to their most per-
-nitious sins, I shall conclude with recommend-
-ing this charity to every on's care, that they do
their utmost to restrain it as well by their owne
Example; as by Precepts, And it may be very

which are free from the Depression of their Trouble, may by an active search find out the most proper means for their Relief.

To those Poor, who have Health and Strength, there is no Charity so beneficial as the keeping them in constant Employment: For if once bestow any such Gifts on them as will incourage their Pride and Sloth, we destroy Industry; Labour will then be irksom to them, and Ruin must follow. Whereas if Youth are betimes enur'd to take some Pains in a busy Life, it will be even burdensome for them to be idle; they should always be persuaded to think Neatness a more becoming Finery, than gaudy Lace and Ribbons: and what Clothing we bestow on them shou'd be fitted more to their necessitys than Fancy.

The putting young Children to School, is a Charity, that, God be prais'd, has prevail'd very much of late; and will, I hope turn to a good account, if not abus'd by too much Pedantry in the Teachers.

As the most profigate Wretches have always charg'd themselves with the Profanation of the Lord's Day, as that which has led to their most pernicious Sins, I shall conclude with recommending this Charity to every one's care, that they do their utmost to **[PP 36]** restrain it, as well by their own Example, as by Precepts: and it may be very

55 (21)

proper to disperse Good Books to this purpose:
for something therein said may happen to touch
them to ye quick, it can scarse be supposed but that
they will gain some farther Advantage by reading
such bookes, then meerly the keeping them so long
? from miss-spending their time; And since the
saving of a Soul is the greatest Benefit any one
is capable of Doing, or Receiving, we certainly
ought to endeavor what in us lies to promote
this Best of all Good Works.

Let none of us think that by Acquiring this Condescending
& Serious Temper, wch I have recommended,
shall either lessen our figure, or deny ourselves
the real injoyments of life; Although we are not
complemented now, True worth will shine forth
& be valued in life, or death, & 'tis a pleasing
reflection to think, Our memory shall smell
sweet, when ye body putrifies; there is
nothing that forbids our Injoying the Innocent
refreshments of this World; But assuredly
in the close of our days there will be no great-
-er Pleasure, then to find we have bin doing
our Duty according to the best of our abilities
wch from an humble heart, will, I trust, through
mercy be acceptable to God; And so may we
finish our course with Joy.

proper to disperse good Books to this purpose; for something therein said may happen to touch them to the quick. It can scarce be suppos'd but that they will gain some further Advantage by reading such Books, than merely the keeping them so long from mispending their time; and since the saving of a Soul is the greatest Benefit any one is capable of doing or receiving, we certainly ought to endeavor what in us lies to promote this best of all good Works.

Let none of us think, that by acquiring this condescending and serious Temper, which I have recommended, we shall either lessen our Figure, or deny our selves the real Enjoyment of Life: altho we are not complemented now, true Worth will shine forth, and be valu'd in Life or Death; and 'tis a pleasing Reflection to think, our Memory shall smell sweet, when the Body putrifies.[43] Yet here is nothing that forbids our enjoying the innocent Refreshments of this World; but assuredly, in the close of our days, there will be no greater Pleasure, than to find we have been doing our Duty, according to the best of our Abilitys; which from an humble Heart will, I trust, thro Mercy, be acceptable to God; and so may we finish our Course with Joy.

Finis

Appendix

Brockman Poem, 1711. Holograph, the Brockman Papers, the British Library, ADD. 42612, dated 1709.

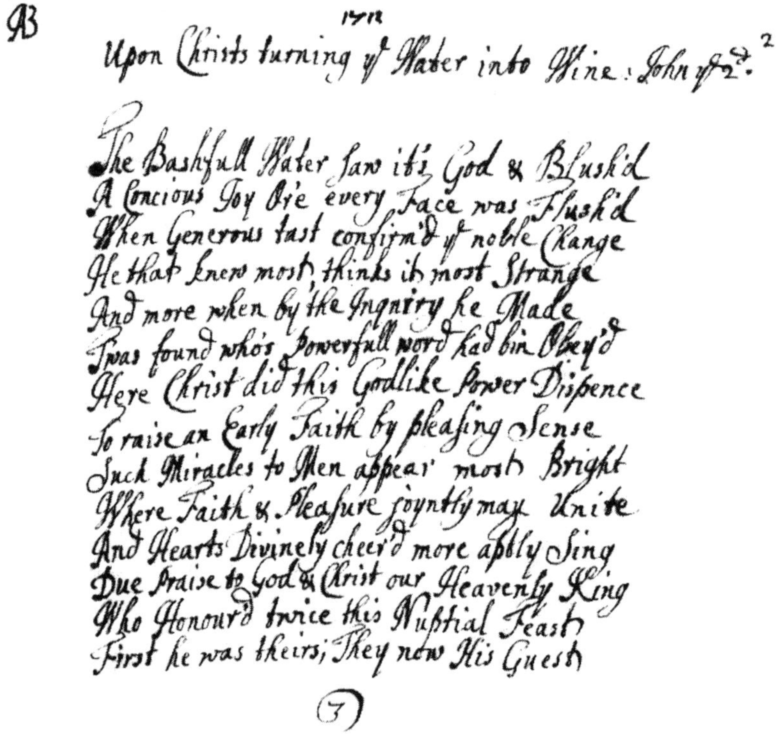

AB

1711

Upon Christs turning ye Water into Wine: John ye 2d.[2]

The Bashfull Water saw it's God & Blush'd
A Concious Joy O're every Face was Flush'd
When Generous tast confirm'd ye noble Change
He that knew most, thinks it most Strange
And more when by the Inquiry he Made
Twas found who's Powerfull word had bin Obey'd
Here Christ did this Godlike Power Dispence
To raise an Early Faith by pleasing Sense
Such Miracles to Men appear most Bright
Where Faith & Pleasure joyntly may Unite
And Hearts Divinely cheer'd more aptly Sing
Due Praise to God & Christ our Heavenly King
Who Honour'd twice this Nuptial Feast
First he was theirs; They now His Guests

(7)

Upon Christ's turning Water into Wine John the Second

The Bashfull Water saw it's God and Blush'd
A Concious Joy Or'e every Face was Flush'd
When Generous last confirm'd the noble Change
He that knew most, thinks it most Strange
And more when by the Inquiry he made
Twas found who's powerfull word had bin Obey'd
Here Christ did this Godlike Power Dispence
To raise an Early Faith by pleasing Sense
Such miracles to Men appear most Bright
Where Faith and Pleasure joyntly may Unite
And Hearts Divinely cheer'd more aptly Sing
Due Praise to God and Christ our Heavenly King
Who Honour's twice this Nuptial Feast
First he was theirs; They now His Guest

Brockman Poem, 1712. Holograph, the Brockman Papers, the British Library, ADD. 42612, dated 1709.

Upon Christs Turning Water into Wine
John ye Second

The Bashfull Water saw it's God & Blush'd
A Concious heat o're every Face was Flush'd
When Generous tast confirm'd ye noble Change
The Governor himself does think it Strange
For finding this ye most Delicious Wine
Why it was keept till now could not Divine
With eager hast a strict Inquirey is Made
And soon they Learn whose Word had bin Obeyed
Thus Christ did his Godlike Power Dispence
To raise an early Faith by pleasing Sense
For Miracles appear to Men most Bright
When Faith & Pleasure joyntly they Excite
And Hearts Divinly cheer'd more aptly Sing
Just Praise to God & Christ our Heavenly King
Who Honouring thus this Nuptial Feast
As he was theirs They now became his Guest

May day
1712

Upon Christ's Turning Water into Wine John the Second

The Bashfull Water san it's God & Bluskd
A concious heat o're every Face was Flush'd
When Generous Fast confirm'd the noble Change
The Governor himself does think it Strange
For finding this the most Delicious Wine
Why it was keept till now cou'd not Divine
With eager hast a strich Inquirey is Made
And soon they Learn whose Word had bin Obayed
Thus Christ did his Godlike Power Dispence
To raise an early Faith by pleasing Sense
For Miracles appear to Men most Bright
When Faith and Pleasure joyntly they Excite
And Hearts Divinly cheer'd more aptly Sing
Just Praise to God and Christ our Heavenly King
Who Honouring thus this Nuptial Feast
As he was theirs They now became his Guest

Mayday
1712[2]

Glydd, Anne. Letter to William Brockman, 1699. The Brockman Papers, the British Library, ADD. 42587.

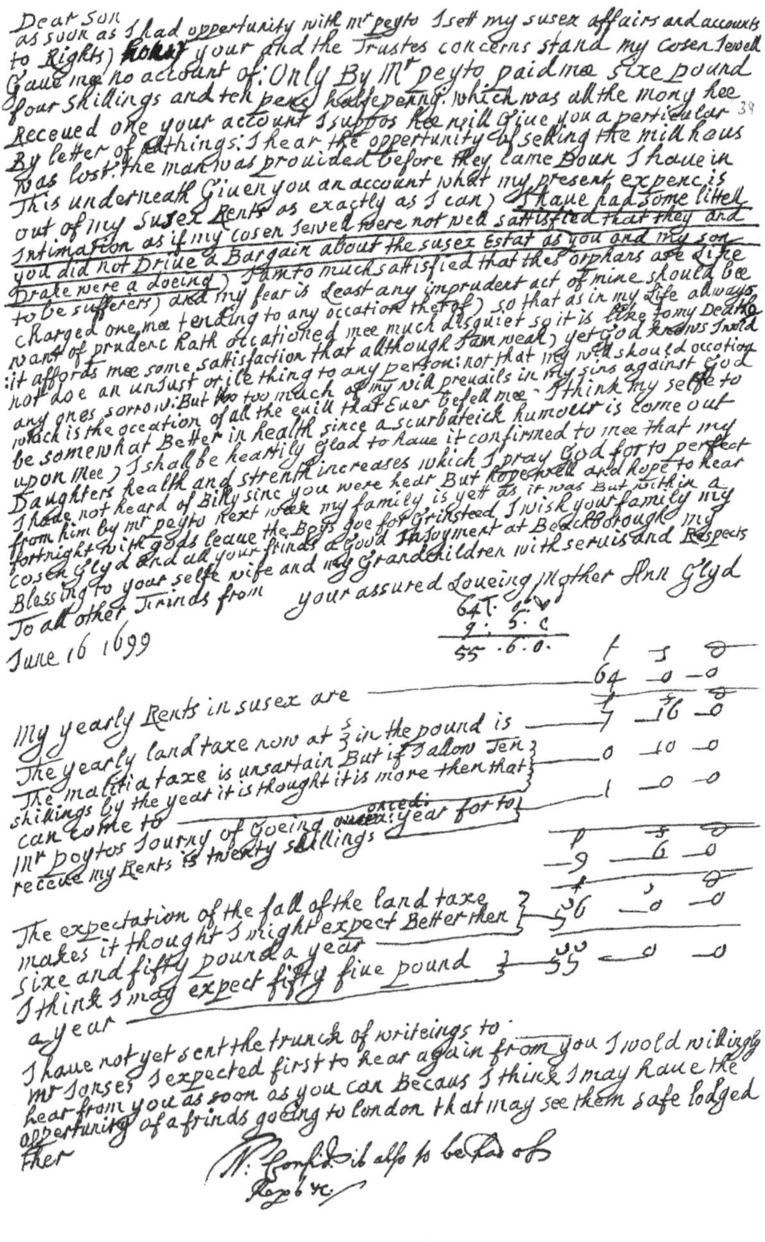

Dear Son
as soon as I had oppertunity with mr peyto I sett my susex affairs and accounts
to Rights) your and the Trustes concerns stand my cosen Jewell
Gaue mee no account of: Only By Mr peyto paid mee sixe pound
four shillings and ten pence halfepenny: which was all the mony hee
Receued one your account I suppos hee will Giue you a perticular 39
By letter of all things: I hear the oppertunity of selling the mill hous
was lost: the man was prouided before they came Doun I haue in
This underneath Giuen you an account what my present expenc is
out of my Susex Rents as exactly as I can) I haue had some littell
Intimation as if my cosen Jewell were not well sattisfied that they and
you did not Driue a Bargain about the susex Estat as you and my son
Drake were a doeing) I am to much sattisfied that the orphans are like
to be sufferers) and my fear is least any imprudent act of mine should bee
charged one mee tending to any occation thereof) so that as in my Life always
want of prudenc hath occationed mee much disquiet so it is like to my Death
:it affords mee some sattisfaction that although I am weak) yet God knows I would
not doe an unjust or ile thing to any person: not that my will should occation
any ones sorrow: But too much of my will preuails in my sins against God
which is the occation of all the euill that Euer befell mee. I think my selfe to
be somewhat Better in health since a scurbateick humour is come out
upon mee) I shall be heartily glad to haue it confirmed to mee that my
Daughters health and strenth increases which I pray God for to perfect
I haue not heard of Billy sinc you were hear But hope well and hope to hear
from him by mr peyto next week my family is yett as it was But within a
fortnight with gods leaue the Boys goe for Grinsteed I wish your family my
cosen Glyd and all your frinds a good Injoyment at Beachborough my
Blessing to your selfe wife and my Grandchildren with seruis and Respects
To all other frinds from your assured Loueing Mother Ann Glyd

June 16 1699

64 . 0 . 0
9 . 5 . 0
55 . 6 . 0

	l	s	d
My yearly Rents in susex are	64	0	0
The yearly land taxe now at 3 in the pound is	7	16	0
The malitia taxe is unsartain But if I allow Ten shillings by the year it is thought it is more then that can come to	0	10	0
Mr poytos Journy of Goeing once a year for to receiue my Rents is twenty shillings	1	0	0
	9	6	0
The expectation of the fall of the land taxe makes it thought I might expect Better then sixe and fifty pound a year	56	0	0
I think I may expect fifty fiue pound a year	55	0	0

I haue not yet sent the trunck of writeings to mr Jonses I expected first to hear again from you I wold willingly hear from you as soon as you can Becaus I think I may haue the oppertunity of a frinds goeing to London that may see them safe lodged ther

[illegible]

Letter to William Brockman from Ann Glydd Sr., 1699.

Dear Son
As soon as I had oppertunity with Mr Peyto I sett my susex affairs and accounts
to Rights how your and the Trustes concerns stand my cosen Jewell
Gaue mee no account of: Only By Mr Peyto paid mee sixe pound
four shillings and ten pen[] halfe penny: which was all the mony hee
Receued one your account I suppos hee will giue you a perticular
By letter of althings: I hear the oppertunity of selling the mill hous
was lost: the man was provided before they came Doun I have in
This underneath given you an account what my present expenc is
out of my susex rents as exactly as I can) I have had some littell
intimation as if my cosen served were not well sattisfied that they and
you did not Driue a Bargain about the susex Estat as you and my son
Drake were a doeing) I am to much sattisfied that thes orphans are like
to be sufferers) and my fears Least and imprudent act of mine should bee
charged one mee tending to any occation therof) so that as in my Life allways
want of prudenc hath occationed mee much disquiet so it is like to my Deathe
:it affords mee some sattisfaction that allthough I am weak, yet God knows I wold
not doe an unjust or ile thing to any person: not that my will should occation
any ones sorrow: But too much of my will prevails in my sins against God
which is the occation of all the euill that Ever befell mee–I think my selfe to
be somewhat Better in health since a scurbuteick humour is come out
upon Mee) I shall be heartily glad to have it confirmed to mee that my
Daughters health and strength increases which I pray God for to perfect
I have not heard of Billy sinc you were hear But hope well and hope to hear
from him by M^{r} peyto next week my family is yett as it was But within a
fortnight with gods leaue the Boys goe for Grinsteed I wish your family my
cosen Glyd and all your frinds a good injoyment at Beachborough my
Blessing to your selfe wife and my grandchildren with servis and respects
To all other Frinds from

your assured Loveing Mother Ann Glyd

June 16 1699

	t	s	o
My yearly rents in susex are	64	0	0
The yearly land taxe now at 3^{S} in the pound is	7	16	0
The malitia taxe is insartain But if I allow Ten shillings by the year it is thought it is more then that can come to	0	10	0
Mr Peytos Journy of goeing onced year for to receue me Rents is twenty shillings	1	0	0
	9	6	0
The expectation of the fall of the land taxe makes it thought I might expect Better then sixe and fifty pound a year	50	0	0

I have not yet sent the trunck of writeings to
Mr Jones I expected first to hear again from you I wold willing
hear from you as soon as you can Becaus I think I may haue the
oppertunity of a frinds goeing to london that may see then safe lodged
ther

Brockman's note
N: [------] it also be has of
[-----] &c[3]

Brockman, Anne. Letter to William Brockman, 1706. The Brockman Papers, the British Library, ADD. 42587.

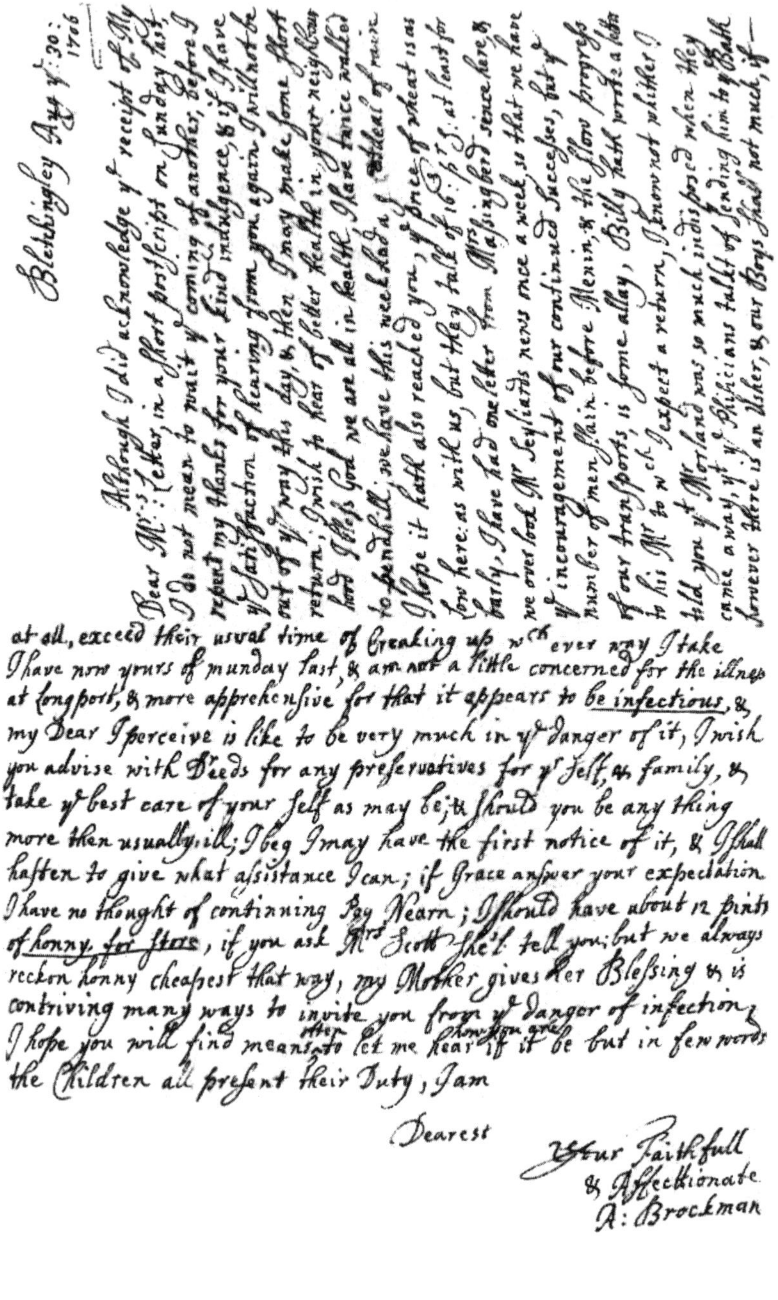

Bletchingley Aug ye: 30: 1706

Dear Mr: Although I did acknowledge ye receipt of My Mr's Letter, in a short postscript on Sunday last, I do not mean to wait ye coming of another, before I repent my thanks for your kind indulgence, & if I have ye satisfaction of hearing from you again I will not be out of ye way this day, & then I may make some short return; I wish to hear of better health in your neighbourhood I bless God we are all in health, I have twice walked to Pendhill, we have this week had a great deal of rain I hope it hath also reached you, ye price of wheat is as low here as with us, but they talk of 16: [?] p: S: at least for barly, I have had one letter from Mrs Massingberd since here & we over look Mr Seyliards news once a week so that we have ye incouragement of our continued Successes, but ye number of men slain before Menin, & the slow progress of our transports, is some allay, Billy hath write a letter to his Mr to wch I expect a return, I know not whither I told you yt Mr Morland was so much indisposed when they came away, yt ye Physicians talkt of sending him to ye Bath however there is an Usher, & our Boys shall not much, if at all, exceed their usual time of breaking up wch ever way I take

I have now yours of munday last, & am not a little concerned for the illness at Longport, & more apprehensive for that it appears to be infectious, & my Dear I perceive is like to be very much in ye danger of it, I wish you advise with Dr Eeds for any preservatives for yr self, & family, & take ye best care of your self as may be; & should you be any thing more then usually ill; I beg I may have the first notice of it, & I shall hasten to give what assistance I can; if Grace answer your expectation I have no thought of continuing Peg Nearn; I should have about 12 pints of honny for store, if you ask Mrs Scott she'l tell you; but we always reckon honny cheapest that way, my Mother gives her Blessing & is contriving many ways to invite you from ye danger of infection; I hope you will find other means to let me hear how you are if it be but in few words the Children all present their Duty, I am

Dearest

Your Faithfull
& Affectionate
A: Brockman

Blenchingly Aug the 30: 1706

Although I did acknowledge the receipt of My
Dear Mrs. Letter, in a short postscript on Sunday last,
I do not mean to wait the coming of another, before I
repeat my thanks for your kind indulgence, & if I have
the Satisfaction of hearing from you again I will not be
out of the way this day, & then I may make some short
return, I wish to hear of better health in your neighbour
-hood, I bless God we are all in health, I have twice walked
to pendhill, we have this week had a good deal of rain
I hope it hath also reached you, the price of wheat is as
Low here as with us, but they talke of 16:^{s} p^{r} L at least for
barly, I have had one letter from Mrs. Assingberd since here, &
we over look Mr. Seylairds news once a week, so that we have
the incouragement of our continued successes, but the
number of men slain before Menin, & the slow progress
of our transports, is some allay, Billy hath wrote a letter
to his Mr. to which I expect a return, I know not whiter I
told you that Mr. Orland was so much indisposed when they
came away, that the Phisicians talkt of sending him to the Bath
however there is an Usher, & our Boys shall not much, if
at all, exceed this usual time of breaking up, which every way I take
I have now yours of munday last, & am not a little concerned for the illness
at Longport, & more apprehensive for that it appears to <u>be infectious</u>, &
my Dear I perceive is like to be very much in the danger of it, I wish
you advise with D^{r}eeds for any preservatives for your self & family, &
take the best care of your self as may be, & should you be any thing
more then usually ill; I beg I may have the first notice of it, & I shall
hasten to give what assistance I can; if Grace answer your expectation
I have no thought of continuing Peg Nearn; I should have about 12 pints
of <u>honny for store</u>, if you ask Mrs. Scott she'l tell you; but we always
reckon honny cheapest that way, my Mother gives her Blessing & is
contriving many ways to invite you from the danger of infection,
I hope you will find means often to let me hear how you are to be but in few words
the Children all present their Duty, I am.

Dearest

Your Faithfull
& Affecttionate
A: Brockman

Brockman, Anne. Letter to Cousin Brockman, 1717. The Brockman Papers, the British Library, ADD. 42588.

Cosin Brockman

May ye 9: 1717
15

The account underwriten I rec'd this day from Mr Brockman with orders to send you a coppy It being a paper wch you signed last June of Mr Randolphs Land Tax Assesments in Aldington for those 2 years, But settled at length according to ye former of ye sd. 2 Rates – And this Mr Brockman desires you may have for yr Direction & Ob-servation Particularly on his account, if ye Assessments are proceeded upon before his return into the country.

1715	£	1716	£	yr Orr: A:B
Herb. Randolph Esqr W: Allen	34	Ditto	38	4 £
Ditto – G Clarke	23	Ditto	26	3
Ditto – Jos: Knight	63	His heires	66	3
				10
Widd Whiting, E Hamon	4	Ditto	3	1
Mr Cade J Clark	4	Ditto	2	2
Widd Hogben	8	Ditto	7	1
Ditto G Wraight	7	Ditto	6	1
Whites heirs J Lawrence	11	Ditto	10	1
J Lilly	3	Sam Lilly	2	1
Mrs Lofty, R Beck	4	Ditto	3	1
Widd. Fagge	6	Ditto	5	1
J. Finis J Howland	3	W. Poden, J Hoskins	3	
Widd. Tomalin	7	Ditto	6	1
				10

Cosin Brockman May the 9: 1717

The account underwritten Ire.[rd] this day
From Mr Brockman with orders to send you a coppy it being
A paper which you signed last June of Mr Randolphs Land Tax
Assesments in Aldington for those 2 years, But sealed att
Length according to the former of the Ld. 2 Rates—And this
Mr Brockman desires you may have for your Direction and Ob-
-Servation Particularly on his account, if the Assessments
are proceeded upon before his return into the country.

1715	Lbra-	1716	L	your clerk A:B
Hest. Randolph Esqr. W.Allen	34	Ditto	38	4—L
Ditto—G Clarke	23	Ditto	26	3
Ditto—Jos. Knight	63	His heires	66	3
				10
Widd Whiting, E Hamon	4	Ditto	3	1
Mr Cade J Clark	4	Ditto	2	2
Widd Hoyben	8	Ditto	7	1
G Wraight	7	Ditto	6	1
Whites heirs I Lawrence	11	Ditto	10	1
Lilly	3	Sam Lilly	2	1
Lofty, R. Beck	4	Ditto	3	1
Fagge	6	Ditto	5	1
Finis J Howland	3	Widden, J Honlan	3	
Widd. Tomalin	7	Ditto	6	1
				10

Brockman, Anne. Letter to William Brockman, 1718. The Brockman Papers, the British Library, ADD. 42588.

Nov: 10 : 1718

My Dear

Coming to spend ye day at Cos: Deedes
at Hythe I meet yrs of ye 3th & they intending for Cant to
to morrow if nott put by as by weather last week, I am
forward to answer yr desire on my thoughts of disposing ye
things at Bletchingly & think it adviseable all should be dis
posed on forthwith reserving only such linnen as is new or
good of ye kind for one use & sheets fit for our servants beds
& that pweter only as I formerly set by what else remain
to be publickly sold & for ye reserved linnen it shoul be put
into one or two of those chests & sent by ye carryer to Lond
& so on to ye green man at Bilingsgate. & I beleive we must
give Neice Patty this aditionall trouble to ye former.
I am glad & pray God to bless yr proceedings for Jack shall
now endeavour to stand prepared for his call to Lond.
Tea is on ye table & chance company come in, & night
hand, I must therefore abruptly with due service to &
from all conclude my self

Yrs Intirly A Brockman

My Dear Nov: 10: 1718

Coming to spend the day at Cos: Deedes
at Hythe I meet them of the 8th and they intending for Cant to
to morrow if not put by as by weather last week, I am
forward to answer your desire on my thoughts of disposing the
things at Bletchingly and think it adviseable all should be dis
posed on forthwith reserving only such linnen as is new or
good of the kind for one use and sheets fit for our servants beds
and that peweter only as I formerly let by what else remain
to be publickly sold for the reserved linnen it should be put
into one or two of those chests and sent by the carryer to Lond
and so on to the green man at Bilingsgate. and I believe we must
give Neice Patty this aditionall trouble to the former.
I am glad and pray God to bless the proceedings for Jack shall
now endeavour to stand prepared for his call to Lond.
Tea is on the table and chance company come in, and night
hand, I must therefore abruptly with due service to and
from all conclude myself

Your Intirly ABrockman

Brockman, Anne. Letter to William Brockman, 1718. The Brockman Papers, the British Library, ADD. 42588.

Beachb Nov: 12
1718

I hope My Dearest will have ye few lines I wrote at Hythe on munday; before this comes to hand with my thoughts as you desiered, that all at Bletchingly should be forthwith disposed on, by publick sale; reserving all ye good linnen, finest table linnen; ye strong & faires sheets, that are fit either for my own, or servants beds, & nothing more; but yt small parcell of pewter wch my Neice Paty knows I formerly set by.
my only 2 journeyes have bin to Aeriss, & Hythe wch were both with saftie; & pleasure, performed with ye old mares, tho not with ye Coachmans likeing, to whom I make no exceptions in ye box; but for ye waiting part, I see little for I have had Beck. for yt purpose ever since you went as they reckon we are a man short in business, for none is yet found thats thought fit for second man, we have a new mate in Robbins room. our servants are 4 of en not free from ailments, but Nick I think by much ye worst, Mr Broom is thought to recover but Mr Colf is very bad. Sr Wm Boys was sent for this day to Mr Honnywood who's feavour lies so much in his head yt he has scatse bin sinsible since Sunday,

Mr Cannon came & lookt on ye wood on Tuesday & was a goodwhile before he could be brought to bid 12£ pr acre. & says now at that price he will take all you sell this year, more he will not give, whither he have it or not, to this, both he, & Young desire yr answer by ye first return to me, Young has bin at Hastingly whence I have yet no mony, but Keeler promises to bring some next week; they say they apprehend some trouble from a Lord, who lais clame to 2 acres of land call'd whitehill, I dont, but perhaps you may understand this story, we have at length got about 80 runts on ye hill but if they go of as quick at ye next, as they did at last fair, we shall not have this prety prospect long,
Mr Rimer, his wife, & Sister all in good health: dined with me on Tuesday; & at ye same time Cos: J. Plumer came & brought me the Scotts: hall anuity from Mr Frankling; with whom he is now a boarder; & under some sort of dejection; having buryed his Mistris but last Saturday, Mr Hodges daughter of Warhorn.
I purpose to morrow to make some inquiry ~~Atte~~ Ratas barly wch I but now heard lies cleand in his floor.

Breach Nov:12 1718
I hope My Dearest will have the few

lines I wrote at Hythe on munday; before this comes to hand with my thoughts as you desired, that all at Bletchingly should be forthwith disposed on, by publick sale; reserving all the good linen, finest table linen; the strong and fairest sheets, that are fit either for my own; or servants beds, and nothing more; but that small parcell of pewter which my Neice Paty knows I formerly set by.
my only 2 journeyes have bin to Acrise, and Hythe; which were both with saftie; and pleasure, performed with the old mares, tho not with the Coachmans likeing, to whom I make no exceptions in the box; but for the waiting part, I see little for I have had Beck. for that purpose ever since you went as they reckon we are a man short in business, for none is yet found thats thought fit for second man, we have a new mate in Robbins room. our servants are 4 ofen not free from ailments, but Nick I think by much the worst, Mr Broom is thought to recover but Mr Colf is very bad. Sir William, Boys was sent for this day to Mr Honnywood who's feavour lies so much in his head that he has leatse bin sensible since Sunday,

Mr Cannon came and lookt on the wood on Tuesday and was a good while before he could be brought to bid 12 pounds per acre. and says now at that price he will take all you sell this year, more he will not give, whither he have it or not, to this, both he, and Young, desire your answer by the first. return to me, Young has bin at Hastingly whence I have yet no mony, but Keeler promises to bring some next week; they say they apprehend some trouble from a Lord, who lais clame to 2 acres of land call'd whitehill, I dont, but perhaps you may understand this story, we have at length got about 80 runts on the hill but if they go of as quick at the next, as they did at last fair, we shall not have this prety prospect long,
Mr Rimer, his wife, and sister all in good health: dined with me on Tuesday; and at the same time Cos: J. Plumer came and brought me the Scotts=hall anuity from Mr Frankling; with whom he is now a boarder; and under some sort of dejection; having buryed his Mistris but last Saturday, Mr Hodges daughter of Warhorn.
I purpose to morrow to make some inquiry After[?] barly which I but now heard lies cleand in his floor.

Pray tell Jemmy I thank him for his letter, & since they make
dificulty of cuting any muslyn; I will wait a little longer, & see if
any of ye late seizure at Hythe wch is just now all condemnd, can be
disposed of in ye country: by permition from above.
Mrs Smith of Hayton spent this day with me; whilst her husband
Jack &c, fetched us a Hare; wch I wish we cou'd have laid at ye feet.
calme open weather: has encouraged going abroad; but it seems
now to be at an end. Mrs Devernex set out on tuesday, & hopes you'l see her.
I presume Mr Hallford will visit you; & tell you his wind-fall by
ye Death of his Kindsman in Warwickshier.
Nick thinks to go to Dover on Satuteday & try to sell wheat.
Brown & W: Macket have bin 2 days at work at Marks at Hythe
on repairs absolutely necessary; wch they say was mentioned to you
tho they had not directly yr orders to do it. they have yet done
little at Beach. the Clock-smith reckons 6d for what he has
done to Mr Staddens clock, wch is in a gainfull way at present, & I
dont well know how to regulate.
my severall respects to yr self, & friends, winds up ye present thoughts of
Jack tenders his Devoir's

yr very Affect. & Faithfull
Wife Brockman

I dont yet hear any thing of ye Hythe boats going to Lond at least till ye condemnd Brandy goes. I beleive Wood has call'd on you this week if he had good luck with his fish.

Drapt-Court
Rd 15 9ber
1718

To

Willm Brockman Esqr at
Mr Blakes in Drapers court
In Princes Street near
Lothbury London

Pray tell Jemmy I thank him for his letter, and since they make
dificulty of cuting any muslyn; I will wait a little longer, and see if
any of the late leizure at Hythe, which is just now Condemnd, can be
disposed of in the country: by permition from ^all above.
Mrs Smith of Hayton spent this day with me; whilst her husband
Jack, and c, fetched us a Hare; which I wish we cou'd have laid at your feet.
calme open weather: has encouraged going abroad; but it seems
now to be at an end. Mrs Devernex set out on tuesday, and hopes you'l see her.
I presume Mr Hallford will visit you; and tell you his wind:fall by
the Death of his Kindsman in Warwickshire.
Nick thinks to go to Dover on Satureday and try to sell wheat.
Brown and W: Macket have bin 2 days at work at Marks at Hythe
on repairs absolutely necesary; which they say was mentioned to you
tho they had not directly your orders to do it. they have yet done
little at Beacht. the clock=smith reckons 650 for what he has
done to Mr Sladdens clock; which is in a gainfull way at present, and I
dont well know how to regulate.
my severall respects to your self, and friends, winds up the present thoughts of

Your very Affect. and Faithfull
Wife ABrockman

Jack tenders his Devour's
I dont yet hear
any thing of the
Hythe boats going
to Lond. at least till
the condemnd Brandy
goes. I believe Wood
has call'd on you
this week if he had
good luck with his
fish.

To
Will[m] Brockman Esqr at
Mr Blakes in Drapers court
In Princes Street near
Lothbury
London
(3)

Brockman, Anne. Letter to James (Jem) Brockman, 1724. The Brockman Papers, the British Library, ADD. 42589.

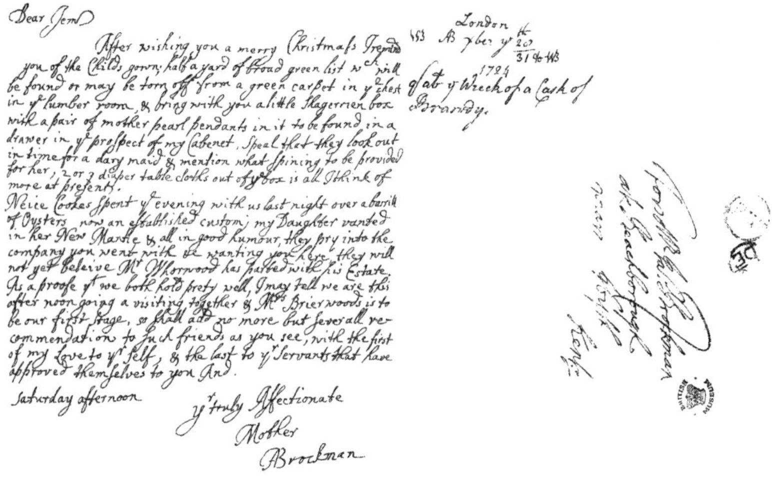

Dear Jem

After wishing you a merry Christmass I remind you of the Childs gown; half a yard of broad green list wch will be found or may be torn off from a green carpet in ye chest in ye lumber room, & bring with you a little Shagerrien box with a pair of mother pearl pendants in it to be found in a drawer in ye prospect of my Cabenet. Speak that they look out in time for a dary maid & mention what spining to be provided for her, 2 or 3 diaper table cloths out of ye box is all I think of more at presents.

Neice Cookes spent ye evening with us last night over a barrill of Oysters now an established custom; my Daughter vanted in her New Mantle & all in good humour, they pry into the company you went with ye wanting you here, they will not yet beleive Mr Whorwood has parted with his Estate. As a proofe yt we both hold prety well, I may tell we are this after noon going a visiting together & Mrs Brierwoods is to be our first stage, so shall add no more but severall recommendation to such friends as you see, with the first of my Love to yr self, & the last to yr Servants that have approved themselves to you And.

Saturday afternoon

yr truly Affectionate
Mother
A Brockman

London
Xber ye 20th
1724
Sat ye Wreck of a Cask of Brandy.

Letter from 1724
Dear Jem,

London

After wishing you a merry Christmas I remind you of the Childs gown; half a yard of broad green list which will be found or may be torn off from a green carpet in the chest in the lumber room, and bring with you a little shagernen box with a pair of mother pearl pendants in it to be found in a drawer in the prospect of my Cabenet, Speak that they look out in time for a dary maid and mention what spinning to be provided for her, 2 or 3 diaper table cloths out of the box is all I think of more at presents.

AB yber youth 200/31 to WB of ab y Wreck of a Cask of Brandy.

Niece Cookes spent the evening with us last night over a barrel of Ousters now an established custom; my Daughter wanted in her New Mantle and all in good humour, they pry into the company you went with etc. wanting you here, they will not yet believe Mr. Whorwook has parted with his Estate.
As a proofe that we both hold prety well, I may tell we are this after noon going a visiting together and Mrs. Brierwoods is to be our first stage, so shall add no more but severall recommendation to such friends as you see, with the first of my Love to your self, and the last to your Servants that have approved themselves to you And.

Saturday afternoon

Your truly Affectionate
Mother
ABrockman

Glydd, Anne. Her Common Book. The Brockman Papers, the British Library, ADD. 45196.

A memorial of our children
births: Sep: 22: 1650

John Glyd borne Sept: 22d: being
Satturday 1650
Elizabeth Glyd borne ye 24th day of
August being ye Lords day 1652 who
lived no longer then til sha was just
7 wekes old
Anne Glyd borne ye 8th of October
1652 who lived no longer til sha was
iust 6 wekes old
Richard Glyd borne ye 26th of
October 1653 being Thursday
Martha Glyd borne ye 10th day of
Februarie 1654 being Satturday
Lawrence Glyd borne ye 2d day of
March 1655 being ye Lordes day
Elizabeth Glyd borne ye 6th of
September 1657 being on ye Lordes day
Anne Glyd borne the 7 of October 1658.....
Being Thursday
My Dearly Beloved Husband Mr
Richard Glyd and Emenant Christan and
and a deare Loueing Loyall exceeding Emenant in the
relation of a husband both to the soul and Body of
mee his wife whos good Councells and instructions if
my god will be pleased to give me the grace to follow I
shall have Cause to Bless my good God to eternety for Him
He Left this Life for a and [illegible] happy Life
the 24 of November 1658 about 5 a clock in the m

A memorial of our children
birthes: Sep: 22: 1650

John Glyd borne Sept: 22: borne, Satturday 1650

Elizabeth Glyd borne the 24th day of August beeing ye Lords day 1651 who lived no Longer then til shee was Just 7 wakes old:

Anne Glyd borne the 8th of October 1652: who Lived no longer til shee was uist 6 weekes old

Richard Glyd borne the 26th of October 1653 beeing Thursday

Martha Glyd borne the 10th day of Februarie 1654 beeing Satturday

Larenee Glyd borne the 2d day of March 1655: beeing the Lordes day

Elizabeth Glyd borne the 6th of September 1657 beeing on the Lordes day

Anne Glyd borne the 7 of October 1658 . . . . . .
Being Thursday

My Dearly Beloved Husband Mr
Richard Glyd and Emenant Christan and
and a deare Loveing Loyall exceeding Emenane in the
relation of a husband both to the soul and Body of
mee his wife whos good Councells and instructions if
my god will be pleased to give me the grace to follow I
shall have Cause to Bless my good God to all eturnetly for Him
the Left this Life for a and eturnal happy Life
the 24 of Nouember 1658 about 5 a clock in the morning

Larenc Glyd Departed This Life may the 3 1659 about 9 at night Being 3 years 2 months and one day old

Richard Glyd Departed this Life June the 13 1662 about 12 a clocke at night being 8 years 7 months and 3 weeks old

Elizabeth Glyd Departed this Life the 7 of nouember: 1681 about 10 a clock in the morning shee was twenty four years and nine weeks lack a day old: A Good and Gratious Child praised be thy name O, my Gratious God for Makeing her such a one

June 12 16[illegible] June 12 1684

in the year of our Lord 1684 My Granddaughter Ann Drake was Borne June the twelfth day being thursday lord my god be pleased two work in her the new birth amen amen: and for Christs sake make her Emenently thy seruant from her infancy amen amen gratious god hear and Grant. She was born about sixe a clock in the Evening

sept 30 1686

My granddaughter Martha Drake was Born the thirtyeth day of September 1686 O my God be pleased so two change her heart and whatever that if it shall please thee two giue her long life shee may dedicate her selfe soul and body two serue thee; and doe thee much eminint seruis in her generation: a Blessed god season her heart with the graces of thy Blessed spirit now in her infancy that shee may serue thee from her youth amen amen amen shee was Born of a thursday about noon baptised the second of october 1686

November 10 1688

the 5 of nou the Prince of orang Began land army My Grandson Ralph Drake was Born the tenth of November 1688 Being satterday Between seven and eaight a clock in the morning shee was baptised the 13 day of November O my God Worke in his heart all the sauing Graces of thy Blessed spirit and make thy holy ordinance of Baptisme Efectuall to him for all thos ends for which thou didst appoint it Amen Amen preserue his life for thy Glory and his relations Comfort and Although hee was born at a time that looked sad and darke and were under Great confussion: yet of thy mercy Be pleased to spare him that hee may liue to see good and Gratious times this church to flourish in peace and holyness

Larene Glyd Departed This Life May the 3 1659 about 9 at night Being 3 years 2 months and one day old

Richard Glyd Departed this Life June the 13 1662
about 12 a cloke at night being 8 years 7 months and 3 weeks

Elizabeth Glyd Departed this Life the 7 of november, 1681
about 10 a clock in the morning shee was twenty four years and nine weeks lack a day old: A Good and Gratious
Child praised be they Name O. My Gratious God for
Makeing her such a one

in the year of our Lord 1684

June 12 1684 June 12 1684
My Granddaughter Ann Drake was Borne June
the twelfth day being thyrsday lord my god be pleased two work in her the new birth amen amen: and for Christs sake make her emenntly thy servant from her infancy amen amen gratious god hear and grant she was born about sixe
a clock in the evening sept 30 1686

My Granddaughter Martha Drake was Born the
thirtyeth day of September 1686 O My God be
pleased so two change her heart and shall ever that if
it shall please thee two give her long life shee may dedicate her selfe soul and body two serve thee: and soe thee much emininet servis in her generation: a Blessed spirit noe in her infancy that shee may serve thee from her youth up amen amen shee was Born of a thursday about noon baptised the
second of october 1686

November 10 1688

the 4 of [ ] the [ ]of [ng] begu Land army

My grandson Ralph Drake was Born the tenth
of November 1688 Being Satterday Between seven
and eight a clock in the Morning He was baptised
the 13 day of November O My God Worke in his heart
ah the saveing Graces of the Blessed spirit and make
thy holy ordinanc of Baptisme Efectual to him for ah
thos ends for which thoe didst appoint it Amen Amen
preserve his Life for thy Glory and his relations Comfort
and Although hee was norn at a time that looked sad and darke and were under great cofusson: yet of they mercy Be pleased to spare him that hee may live to see good and gratious times thy church to flourish in peace and hollyness[4]

Nouember 23 1689

My Dearly Beloued and Extryordinary Dutifull
son John Glyd Departed this life Nouember 23
1689 about foo a clock in the morning: being
nine and thirty year old the 21 of september before
hee was usefull in his Genaration to man: and truly
serued god in his genaration O My God help
mee his sorrowfull Mother to Rest sattiefied
with thy will: Dr hampton preached his funarol sermon
his text was Philippians 1: vers 21 For to mee to liue is Christ and
to die is Gain

August 4 1690 my Daughter Drake was Brough abed of a second
son who was baptized the 7 instant and named John in remembranc
of his uncle John Glyd the Lord make him to liue his Good life and furnish him
with all gifts and graces that he may be an emmenat instrument of Gods glory
and true Good to himself and others souls and Bodys

June 8 1692 my Daughter Drake was Brought abed of a Daugher named
Elizabeth in rememberanc of her Aunt Elizabeth Glyd the Lord Make
her to follow her Good life growing in grace in wisdome and in
understanding and fauus with god and man and haue comfart in this life and
happiness in the liue to come be a father and mother to her who neuer remember
any Earthly ones

Aprill 23 1694 my Daughter Drake was brought abed of a Daughter
who was named sarah in Respect to her Cosen Sarah Stoughton
The Lord make her emenent in all Gifts and Graces for his Glory and
her comfart one Earth and Euerlasting happines in mercy take care of them
the fatherless findeth mercy Be ther father who neuer knew father nor mother

July 31 1694 my Daughter Drake dye of the smalpoxe Being the
fortyeth year of her age shee was uertious pious Good woman shee
Left sixe smal children Behind her the Lord in mercy take care of them
and bestow one them al what is truely good for ther souls and bodys

July 13 1695 my Son Drake Dyed and Left the sixe children
Behind him which his wife Left and now that father and Mother
hath left them Good God for Christs sake take them up into care and
prouide for them what Euer thou knowest to be Good for their souls
and Body 68

July 28 1695 my son Drake being dead I came to his hous to try what
I could be assisting in for Good ther poor 6 orphans my Grandchildren
I was frustrated much in my thoughts by the unkind and I may say Euile
carridg of ther trusties to mee: But trusing to the Almighty haueing noe
Euill ends: But a hearty desire to doe them Good souls and bodys and doe
my duty my God hath wonderfully helped thee this year and allmost a
Halfe it being now nouember 24 1697 O lord my God euer asiste in my
Duty to thee my god and man keep thee in my right reson and true
understanding and spare my life so long as I am able truly set se
and pleas thee and be usefull for the true good of the souls and
Bodys of thes orphans recc ue rise to thy men— through
the merits of thy son when I breath out
my soul

My Dear son John Glyd was Born September
the one an twenty being satterday in the year 1650.

November 23 1689
My Dearly Beloved and Extryordinary Dutiful
son John Glyd Departed this life November 23
1689 about too a clock in the morning: being
nine and thirty year old the 21 of september before
hee was usefull in his Genaration to man: and truly
served God in his Genaration (,) My God help
mee his sorrowful Mother to Rest sattiefied
with thy will : Dr. hampton preached his funeral sermon
his text was Philippans 1: uers 21 For to mee to live is Christ and
to die is Gain.

August 4, 1690 My Daughter Drake, was Brough abed of a second
son who was baptized the I instant and named John in rememberanc
of his uncle John Glyd the Lord make him to know his God Life and furnish him
with all gifts and graces that he may be an emmenat instrument of Gods glory
and true Good to himself and others Souls and Bodys

June 8 1692 My Daughter Drake was Brought abed of a Daughter named
Elizabeth in remembrenc of her Aunt Elizabeth Glyd the Lord make
her to follow her Good Life growing in Grace in wisdome and in
understanding and focus with God and man and have comfort in this life and
happiness in the live to come be a father and mother to her who neuer remember
any earthly ones

April 23 1694 My Daughter Drake was brought abed of a Daughter
who was named Sarah in Respect to her cosen Sarah Stoughton
the Lord make her emenent in all Gifts and Graces for his Glory and
her comfart one Earth and Euerlasting happines mercy take care of them
the fatherless Findeth mercy Be ther father who neuer knew father nor mother
July 31, 1694 my Daughter Drake dye of the small poxe Being the
Fortyeth-year of her age shee was a uertious pious Good woman shee
Left sixe small children behind her the Lord in mercy take care of them
and bestow one them all what is truely Good for ther souls and bodys

July 13. 1695 My son Drake Dyed and left the sixe children
Behind him which his wife left and now that father and mother
hath left them Good God for Christs • sake take them up into care and
provide for them what Euer thou know'est to be Good for their souls
and Body 68

July 20 1695 My son Drake being dead I came to his house to try what
I could be assisting in for Good ther poor G orphans my Grandchildren
I was frustrated much in my thoughts by the unkind and I may say Euile
carnidy of ther trusties to mee: But trusing to the Almighty haueing noe
Euill Ends: But a hearty desire to doe thee in Good souls and bodys and doe
My duty my God hath wonderfully helped thee this year and almost a
Halfe it being now nouember 24, 1697 O lord my God euer asiste in my
Duty to thee my God and man Keep thee in my rightoeson and true
understanding and spare my Life so long as I am able truly setle
and please thee and be usefull for the true good of the soul's and
Body of thes orphans reccue rise to thy men—through
the merits of thy son when I breath out
my soul

Hee Left 6 small Children Behind him The Eldest
of Them Being But 8 year olde and 9 weekes
The youngest of Them but 6 weeks and 6 days old
whom I beleue my good for god for his mercy and
my blessed saviours Chrets sake as thee hath bine
Grasously pleased to be both Father and
mother unto mee will be so to them if they beleue
in him which beleue good god contine mee in and
worke in them
[illegible]
[illegible]
to beleue
My Dear Husband allways laboured firmly
to beleue that all the promises in the Gospell
made to the rightous and ther seede shall
at one time or other be made good to him
and his seed now I bessech my good god to
inabell mee whill I liue to beleue this and giue
them grace my good god I intreat thee firmly to
beleue in thee and to kole them selfes one
thy promises and all things our Blesed
Saviour hath told us is possiabell to faith
and as my deare husband wold often
when at any time hee stired mee up to beleue
tell mee that unbeleuf was the daming sin
and if once wee could but heartily
beleue all other sins wold be pardoned
and grace wold flow in to our hartes
for unbeleue hinders all good from us my Dear
Children let this thinge be remembered by you
when my body shall be desouled into Dust that you
had a Father whom if he should Haue Lived to haue
sen you Children of unbeleue wold haue as much as in
him lay haue hindered you of the good things of this
Life and shall at the day of Judgment resoyce in you
Just condemnation if you should be wicked wretches
O my Dear Children fear and trembell and beg of
god one your knees that hee wold giue you grace to
fear him that god your maker and now your father
may not pronounce that sentene a ganst you Depart you
cursed into hell fier prepared for the Divell and his
angells

Hee Left 6 small Children Behind him The Eldest
of them Being But 8 years old and 9 weekes
the youngest of Them but 6 weeks and 6 days old
whom I beleve my good for god for his mercy and
my blessed savours [vets] sake as hee hath bine
Grasously pleased to be both Father and
mother unto mee will be so to them if they beleve
in him which beleve good god conti[——e] mee in and
worke in them
[TWO LINES ARE CROSSED OUT AND NOT READABLE ~~to belive~~]
My Dear Husband allways Laboured firmly
to beleve that all the promises in the gospell
made to the rightous and ther seed should
at one time or other be made good to him
and his seed now I bessech my good god to
inabell mee whill I live to beleve this and give
them grace my good god I intreat thee firmly to
beleve in thee and to Role them selfes one
thy promises and all things our Blesed
savour hath told us is possibell to faith
and as my deare husband wold often
when at any time hee stired mee up to beleve
tell mee that unbeleus was the daming sin
and if once wee ~~up~~ could but heartyly
beleve all other sins wold be pardoned
and grace wold flow in to our hartes
for unbeleve hinders all good from us my Dear
children Let this thinge ~~bevement~~ be remembered by you
when my body shall be desouled into Dust that you
had a Father whom if he should Have Lived to a have
sen you Children of unbeleve wold have as much as in
him Lay have hindered you of the good things of this
Life and shall at the day of Juddgment rejoyce in you
just condemnation if you should be wicked wretches
O My Dear Children hear and membell and beg of
god one your knees that hee wold give your grace to
hear him that God your maker and man your father
may not pronounce that sentence a ganst you Depart you
cursed into hell fier prepared for the Diuell and his
angels[5]
Glyd, mother of Ann Glyd Brockman

December 22 1692 my Dear Daughter Ann Glyd
was married To Willam Brockman Esqr O Lord it may
Grant
Draue to Both ther Comforts in this life [illegible] heauenly much
more Let it Conduce to the good of ther souls that may help one
another in the way to heauen Bee suitabel help meets Both for the
good of ther soules and Bodys

my Grandson Willam Brockman was Born
December 26 1693 my Grandson ... one St Steuens day
about four a clock in the morning one St Steuens day
it Being one a tuasday O Lord saintifie him that
hee may Be thy faithfull fruitfull saruant heare one
the Earth and a Glorified saint for euer with in heauen
after a long and weed spent life one Earth

my Grandson James Brockman was Born
October 27 1696 about fiue a clock in the morning it Being tuasday
Almighty God regenerate him that
for Christ Jesus sake that he may become thy True and faithfull saruant and
Hee may become thy True and faithfull saruant and Comefartable Life hear
after a Long and wed spent Comefartable Life hear
one Earth hee may Raign with thee in euerlasting
Felicity in Heauen

December 22 1692 My Dear Daughter Ann Glyd
was married to Willam Brockman Esqr O Lord Grant it may
praye to Both ther comforts in this life [?] heavenly much
more let it conduce to the Good of ther souls that may help one
another in the way to heaven Bee suitable help meets Both for the
good of ther souls and Bodys

December 26, 1693 My Grandson Willam Brockman was Born
about four a clock in the morning one St Stevens day
it Being one a tuesday O Lord saintific Him that
hee may Be thy faithfull fruitfull sarvant herer one
the Earth and a Glorified saint for euer with thee in heaven
after a long and []ed spent life one Earth

October 27 1696 My Grandson James Brockman was Born
about five a clock in the morning it Being tuasday
For Christ Jesus sake Almighty God regenerate him that
Hee may become they True and faithfull sarvant and
after a Long and wed spent comefartable Life hear
one Earth hee may Raign with thee in Everlasting
Felicity in Heaven[6]

Notes

Introduction

1. James, Fitzmauice, gen. ed. and Josephine A. Roberts, textual ed. *Major Women Writers of Seventeenth-Century England*. Ed. Carol L. Barash, Eugene R. Cunnar, and Nancy A. Gutierrez, Ann Arbor, MI: University of Michigan Press, 1997, 2.
2. This refers to the literary war fought in printed tracts about the nature of women. The debate began in the mid-sixteenth century and continued for nearly a century. Jane Anger, Rachel Speght, and Esther Sowernan were some of the main female responders. To sell more pamphlets, some of the tracts involved in the debate were written and then answered by the same person using another pen name.
3. Anne Brockman. *Age Rectified*. London, 1709, 7.
4. Members of the lower classes usually lived in nuclear family units. Children left to find jobs and then begin families away from their parents.

1 Mothers, Wives, Widows, and Mother's Advice Books of the Seventeenth Century

1. Suzanne W. Hull. *Chaste, Silent & Obedient: English Books for Women, 1475–1640*. San Marino, CA: Huntington Library, 1982, 17–18.
2. Lawrence Stone. *The Family, Sex and Marriage: In England 1500–1800*. New York: Harper & Row Publishers, 1977, 51.
3. Edward Wrigley and Roger Schofield. *The Population History of England 1541–1871: A Reconstruction*. Cambridge, MA: Harvard University Press, 1981, 234.
4. Keith Wrightson. *Earthly Necessities; Economic Lives in Early Modern Britain*. New Haven, CT: Yale University Press, 2000, 229.
5. Mary Abbot. *Life Cycles in England, 1560–1720: Cradle to Grave*. London: Routledge, 1996, 26.
6. Keith Wrightson. *English Society 1580–1680*. New Brunswick, NJ: Rutgers University Press, 1982, 105.

7. Stone. *The Family, Sex and Marriage*, 72.
8. Roger Finlay. *Population and Metropolis: the Demography of London, 1580–1650*. Cambridge, England: Cambridge University Press, 1981, 108.
9. Abbot. *Life Cycles*, 135.
10. David I. Kertzer and Peter Laslett (*Aging in the Past: Demography, Society, and Old Age*. Berkeley: University of California Press, 1995) do not state male/female life expectancy figures until the 1880s when more detailed records exist. This practice is common in many demographic texts concerning this point. Sarah Mendelson and Patricia Crawford use S. R. Johnson's, "Welfare, Mortality, and Gender: Continuity and Change in Explanation for Male/Female Differences over Three Centuries." *Continuity and Change* 6 (1991): 135–177, for their estimation of women's life expectancy.
11. Sara Mendelson and Patricia Crawford. *Women in Early Modern England 1550–1720*. Oxford, England: Clarendon Press, 1998, 194.
12. Anne Laurence. *Women in England 1500–1760: A Social History*. New York: St. Martin's Press, 1994, 28.
13. Laurence. *Women in England*, 29.
14. Stone. *The Family, Sex and Marriage*, 58.
15. Ibid., 79.
16. Jacques Guillemeau. *Child-Birth, or the Happy Deliverie of Women* (STC 12496, 1616), 86.
17. David Cressy. *Birth, Marriage, and Death: Ritual, Religion, and the Life-Cycle in Tudor and Stuart England*. Oxford, England: Oxford University Press, 1997, 30.
18. Roger Schofield. "Did the Mothers Really Die? Three Centuries of Maternal Mortality in The World We Have Lost." *The World We Have Gained*. Ed. Lloyd Bonfield, Richard M. Smith, and Keith Wrightson. Oxford, England: Oxford University Press, 1986, 231–260.
19. Lucinda McCray Beier. *Sufferers & Healers: The Experience of Illness in Seventeenth Century England*. London: Routledge & Kegan Paul, 1987, 135.
20. Mendelson and Crawford. *Women in Early Modern England*, 152.
21. Lexis-Nexis Statistical Universe-Document. March 8, 2002. <http://web.lexisnexis.com/statuniv/document?_m=c720545b266cbf9c0bb665f4ebe52106& . . .>
22. Lexis-Nexis Statistical Universe-Document. March 8, 2002. <http://web.lexis-nexis.com/statuniv/document?_m=64eb42427aa265159d8bf285b67c7260& . . .>
23. Dorothy McLaren. "Marital Fertility and Lactation 1570–1720." *Women in English Society, 1500–1800*. Ed. Mary Prior. London: Methuen, 1985, 22.
24. Cressy, *Birth, Marriage, and Death*, 21.
25. Ibid., 24.
26. Laura Growing. *Common Bodies: Women, Touch & Power in 17th Century England*. New Haven. CT: Yale University Press, 2003, 200.
27. McLaren. "Marital Fertility," 23. Breast-feeding causes the pituitary gland to secrete prolactin, which both promotes the production of milk and inhibits the ovarian function (researchers debate the degree of contraception). Although this process was not understood during the seventeenth century, there was some understanding about the connection between breast-feeding and contraception.

28. Cressy. *Birth, Marriage, and Death*, 87.
29. John Sadler. *The Sicke Womans Private* (STC 21544, 1636), 10.
30. Merry E. Wiesner. *Women and Gender in Early Modern Europe*. 2nd Ed. Cambridge, England: Cambridge University Press, 2000, 87.
31. Growing, *Common Bodies*, 198–199.
32. The Countess of Lincoln implies that the choice to hire a wet nurse was not her own, but of one who had power over her—her husband, perhaps?
33. Of particular interest is the belief the good qualities are transferred from mother to child, and the belief that a wet nurse could transfer bad qualities to the child.
34. Eucharius Roesslin. *The Birth of Man-kinde; Otherwise Named the Womans Book*. Tr. Thomas Raynold (STC 21161, 1604), 161.
35. Jane Sharpe. *Midwives Book: Or the Whole Art of Midwifery Discovered.* (1671).
36. *Birth. Marriage, and Death*. [Cressy quotes Henry New come]
37. McLaren. *Birth, and Marriage, and Death*, 25.
38. Sharp. *Midwives Book*, 365–5.
39. McLaren. *Marital Fertility*, 45.
40. Laslett. *Aging in the Past*, 35.
41. C. W. Chalklin. *Seventeenth-Century Kent: A Social and Economic History*. London: Longmans, 1965.
42. Wrightson. *English Society*, 111, 29.
43. Ibid., 24.
44. Laslett, *Aging in the Past*, 66.
45. Ibid., 34.
46. Wrightson. *English Society*, 87.
47. Laslett. *Aging in the Past*, 86.
48. Chalkin. *Seventeenth-Century Kent*, 28.
49. Ibid., 28, 191, and 198.
50. Ibid., 210.
51. Drake-Brockman, family tree.
52. Wrightson. *Earthly Necessities*, 162.
53. Celia Fiennes. *The Journeys of Celia Fiennes*. Ed. Christopher Morris. London: The Cresset Press, 1949, 124. The expansion of industry can be seen in Celia Fiennes's entry in her private journal. While on a tour of Kent in 1697, Celia Fiennes described the paper mill she visited:

    > There are also Paper mills which dispatches paper at a quick rate; they were then marketing brown paper when I saw it; the mill is set agoing by the water and at the same tyme it pounded the rags to morter for the paper, and it beate oatmeale and hemp and ground bread together that is at the same tyme; when the substance for the paper is pounded enough they take it in a great tub and so with a frame just of the size of the sheetes of paper, make all of small wire just as I have seen fine screens to screen corne in, only this is much closer wrought, and the clap a frame of wood round the edge, and so dip it into the tub and what is too thinn runs through; then they turn this frame down on a piece of coarse woollen just of the size of the paper and so give a knock to it and it falls off, on which they clap

> another such a piece of woollen cloth which is ready to lay the next frame of paper, and so till they have made a large heape which they by an board on the bottom move to a press, and so lay a board on the top and so let down a great screw and weight on it, which they force together into such a narrow compass as they know so many sheetes of paper will be reduced, and this presses out all the thinner part and leaves the paper so firme as it may be taken up sheete by sheete, and laid together to be thoroughly dryed by the wind; they told me white paper was made in the same manner only they must have while woollen to put between; there is a great number of French people in this town which are employ'd in the weaving and silk winding. . . .

Celia Fiennes (1662–1741) traveled throughout England from 1691 to 1703. She kept a personal journal, and in 1948, it was published as *The Journeys of Celia Fiennes*. Fiennes, like many women of the period, wrote privately with no thought of publishing her journal, although it did circulate among friends. Fiennes was a nonconformist who saw nothing wrong with friends and family members marrying tradesmen. Indeed, Fiennes enjoyed moving freely between the two social groups. Unlike the women who wrote mother's advice books, Fiennes did not feel she had to stay within the bounds of femininity or her roles in society, and her social position allowed her to express her views. Fiennes had an interest in mining, drainage projects, and manufacturing processes, and her interest in manufacturing can be seen by her attention to detail as she describes papermaking. Like Anne Brockman, what we know about Fiennes must be gleaned from her written record that she has left behind.

54. Claire S. Schen. "Strategies of Poor Aged Women and Widows in Sixteenth-Century London." *Women and Ageing in British Society Since 1500*. Ed. Lynn Botelho and Pat Thane. London: Pearson Education, 2001, 15.
55. Ibid., 16.
56. Lynn Botelho and Pat Thane, eds. "Introduction." *Women and Ageing in British Society Since 1500*. London: Pearson Education, 2001, 49.
57. Gregory King. *Natural and Political Observations*, 1696, 40.
58. L. A. Botelho. "Images of Old Age in Early Modern Cheap Print: Women, Witches, and the Poisonous Female Body." *Power & Poverty: Old Age in Pre-Industrial Past*. Ed. Susannah R. Ottaway, L. A. Botelho, and Katherine Kittredge. Westpoint, CN: Greenwood Press, 2002, 4.
59. Ibid., 229.
60. Ibid., 231–232.
61. Ibid., 236.
62. Ibid., 236.
63. Arthur C. Danto. *The Madonna of the Future: Essays in a Pluralistic Art World*. New York: Farrar, Straus, and Giroux, 2000, 156. Danto believes that Anguissola's move from her family to the Spanish court was not artistically advantageous for her. The official portraits adhered to the somewhat rigid Spanish taste, and "there was little outlet for her comic spirit of *The Chess Game*," an early painting of her sisters playing chess.

64. Frances Borzello. *Seeing Ourselves: Women's Self-Portraits*. London: Harry N. Abrams, Inc., Publishers, 1998, 49.
65. Mendelson and Crawford. *Women in Early Modern England*, 187.
66. Borzello, *Seeing Ourselves*, 49.
67. Ibid., 46.
68. Mendelson and Crawford. *Women in Early Modern England*, 191.
69. Alan Macfarlane. *Marriage and Love in England: Modes of Reproduction 1300–1840*. Oxford, England: Basil Blackwell, 1986, 109.
70. Mendelson and Crawford, *Women in Early Modern England*, 191.
71. Macfarlane, *Marriage and Love in England*, 110.
72. J. A. Sharpe. *Early Modern England: A Social History 1550–1760*. London: Edward Arnold, 1987, 70.
73. See Sharpe. *Early Modern England*; Wrightson, *English Society 1580–1680*; Wiesner, *Women and Gender in Early Modern Europe*; and Alan Macfarlane, *Marriage and Love in England* to name a few.
74. Wrightson. *English Society*, 106, 116.
75. Macfarlane, *Marriage and Love in England*, 52.
76. Wiesner. *Women and Gender*, 92.
77. Peter Laslett, ed. *Household and Family in Past Time*. Cambridge, England: Cambridge University Press, 1972, 58.
78. Anne Brockman. *Age Rectified*. London: 1709, 34.
79. Ralph Houlbrooke. *The English Family: 1450–1700*. London: Longman, 1984, chapter 5.
80. Brockman, *Age Rectified*, 16.
81. Anne Llewellyn Barstow. *Witchcraze: A New History of the European Witch Hunts*. New York: Pandora, 1995, 27.
82. These stock characters were in such abundance during the Restoration that it is impossible to list them all. The most famous and most reprinted play of this kind is William Wycherley's *The Country Wife*.
83. Since many of the marriages between old men and young women were financial deals, perhaps, "buying" would be a better term than "winning."
84. William Congreve. *The Way of the World. Restoration and Eighteenth-Century Comedy*, 2nd ed. Ed. Scott McMillian. New York: Norton & Co., 1973; 1997, 272.
85. Susanna Fesserson. *A Bargain for Bachelors Or: The Best Wife in the World for Penny*. E. A., 1675.
86. Ibid.
87. Ibid., 5.
88. Ibid., 4.
89. Ibid., 8.
90. Anne Kugler. " 'I feel myself decay apace': Old Age in the Diary of Lady Sarah Cowper (1644–1720)." *Women and Ageing in British Society Since 1500*. Ed. Lynn Botelho and Pat Thane London: Pearson Education, 2001, 73.
91. Thomas Becon. *The Catechism*. Cambridge: University Press, 1844, 348.
92. A through discussion of this ideal is Ian Maclean's *The Renaissance Notion of Woman: A Study in the Fortunes of Scholarticism and Medical Science in*

European Intellectual Life. Cambridge, England: Cambridge University Press, 1980.

93. For a discussion of parental advice books see Judith Gero John "Commands and Whispers: Renaissance Parental Advice Books, Their Tradition, and Their Value in Literary Studies." Kansas: Diss. Kansas State University, 1992.
94. For an educational and entertaining view of what men have to say about women in Tudor and Stuart publications, see Suzanne W. Hull. *Women According to Men: The World of Tudor-Stuart Women*. London: AltaMira Press, 1996. For a discussion of self-discipline evident in prisons and prisoners, see Michel Foucault. *Discipline and Punish: The Birth of the Prison*. New York: Vintage/Random House, 1979.
95. Ann Rosalind Jones, "Surprising Fame: Renaissance Gender Ideologies and Women's Lyric." *The Poetics of Gender*. Ed. Nancy K. Miller. New York: Columbia University Press, 1986, 79.
96. Randall Martin, ed. *Women Writers in Renaissance England*. London: Longman, 1997, 2.
97. Patricia Crawford. "Women's Published Writings 1600–1700." *Women in English Society 1500–1800*. Ed. Mary Prior. London: Methuen, 1985, 213.
98. Sharpe. *Early Modern England*, 278. These estimations are based on the ability and opportunity to sign one's name. It is difficult to estimate how many people could only sign their name and those who could sign and write more extensively. Also there is no way to know who could sign their name but were not given the opportunity to do so i.e. someone who did not own land or had a small amount of possessions had no reason to sign documents unless as a witness or if embroiled in some legal dispute.
99. Sharpe. *Early Modern England*, 279.
100. Frances Teague. "Judith Shakespeare Reading." *Shakespeare Quarterly*. 47.4 (1996): 372.
101. Sidney was so popular that his death was considered a great loss to English poetry. Additionally, his sister, Mary Sidney and niece, Lady Mary Wroth were well-known for their poetry and translations via manuscript circulation before they published any of their work.
102. The Statute of Queen Anne, 1710, created the first modern copyright system, recognizing authors as the primary beneficiary of the monopoly rights granted by a copyright. The other important thing the Statute of Queen Anne did was to make copyright a *limited* monopoly right (fourteen years with the option of renewing for another fourteen years), after which a work passed into the Public Domain.
103. On of the most famous comedies to play with this ideal of silent woman is Ben Jonson's popular play *Epiocene, or the Silent Woman*, 1609. Morose is a gentleman who loves silence, and his extreme rejection of noise enables him to be tricked into marrying a "silent woman" (this terminology misses on both counts when the bride unveils herself as a talkative man).
104. Crawford. "Womens Published Writings," 217.
105. Aphra Behn, one of the most famous playwrights of the seventeenth century, was often chastised for writing. In her address to the reader before *Sir Patient Fancy*, 1678, Behn charges that her work is no more bawdy than the popular

plays by men. She stands accused of bawdiness because the critics consider it unnatural for a woman.

106. Bell's work is reminiscent of the medieval account of a woman's life *The Book of Margery Kempe* (1500). Visions also help her find her spiritual way through life. Unlike Bell, Kempe could not write, so she was forced to tell her story to a monk who wrote it for her. How this affected the final work is unknown.
107. Abbot. *Life Cycles in England*, 26. The mortality rate of London was higher than rural areas for an assortment of reasons including fresh air and food, less sewerage, a smaller population, and cleaner water.
108. Elizabeth Grymeston. *Miscelanea, Meditations, Memoratiues*. London, 1604, A3.
109. Ibid., B2v.
110. Ibid., A3.
111. Ibid., B1v.
112. Elaine V. Beilin. "Redeeming Eve: Defenses of Women and Mother's Advice Books." *Redeeming Eve: Women Writers of the English Renaissance*. Princeton: Princeton University Press, 1987, 269.
113. Grymeston. *Miscelanea*, A3.
114. Ibid., B2.
115. Grymeston. "Chapter 17." *Miscelanea, Meditations, Memoratives*. Martin, ed. *Women Writers in Renaissance England*, 115.
116. Grymeston. *Miscelanea*, 116.
117. Martin. *Women Writers*, 98.
118. Cressy. *Literacy and the Social Order*. Cambridge: Cambridge University Press, 1980, 176.
119. Dorothy Leigh. *The Mothers Blessing or The Godly Counsil of a Gentlewoman Not Long Since Deceased, Left Behind for Her Children*. London: John Pudge, 1616, A2.
120. Ibid., A7r.
121. Ibid., 4.
122. Ibid., 15–16.
123. Ibid., 49
124. Ibid., 54.
125. Ibid.
126. Ibid., 55.
127. Ibid.
128. Ibid., 62.
129. Ibid., 63.
130. Ibid., 30.
131. Ibid., 35.
132. Ibid., 35–36.
133. Ibid., 37.
134. Ibid., 39–40.
135. Suzanne W. Hull. *Chaste, Silent & Obedient*, 63. Quoted from the Lawes Resolutions of Womens Rights: or, the Lawes Provision for Women (1632).
136. Leigh. *The Mothers Blessings*, 39.

137. Roger Schofield. "Did the Mothers Really Die?" 236.
138. Martin. *Women Writers*, 35.
139. Elizabeth Josceline. *The Mothers Legacy to her Unborn Childe*. Ed. Jean Le Drew Metcalfe. Toronto: University of Toronto Press, 2000, 8–10 [line numbers will be used to cite this work].
140. Goad, 37–40.
141. Jean Le Drew Metcalfe, ed. "The Introduction," *The Mothers Legacy to her Unborn Childe*, 3.
142. Goad, Thomas. "The Approbation." Elizabeth Josceline, *The Mothers Legacy to her Unborn Childe*. Ed. Jean Le Drew Metcalfe, 53–55
143. Joceline, "To my truly louinge and most Dearly loued husband Taurell Jocelin," *The Mothers Legacy to her Unborn Childe*, 14–16.
144. Ibid., 20–34.
145. Ibid., 38–52.
146. Ibid., 54–58.
147. Ibid., 62–67.
148. Ibid., 79.
149. Weisner. *Women and Gender in Early Modern Europe*, 87.
150. Elizabeth Clinton. *The Countesse of Lincolnes Nurserie*. Oxford: John Lichfield and James Short, 1628, A2.
151. Ibid., A2v
152. Ibid., A4.
153. Ibid., B.
154. Ibid., B3.
155. Ibid., C4–C4v.
156. Wiesner, *Women and Gender in Early Modern Europe*, 87.
157. Thomas Brooks. "Introduction." *The Legacy of a Dying Mother to Her Mourning Children, Being the Experiences of Mrs. Susanna Bell, Who Died March 13, 1672*, Mrs. Susanna Bell, London: John Hancock, 1673, 42.
158. Susanna Bell, *The Legacy of a Dying Mother to Her Mourning Children, Being the Experiences of Mrs. Susanna Bell, Who Died March 13, 1672*, 44.
159. Ibid., 60.
160. Ibid., 61.
161. Elizabeth Richardson. *A Ladies Legacy to her Daughters*. Ed. Charlotte F. Otten, Miami: Florida International University Press, 1992, 304.
162. Virginia Woolf. *A Room of One's Own*. New York: Harcourt Brace & Company, 1981, 1929.

2 The Author and the Text

1. David Henry Drake-Brockman. *Record of the Brockman and Drake-Brockman Family*. Lindsfield, Sussex, England: D. H. Drake-Brockman, 1936.
2. J. A. Sharpe. *Early Modern England: A Social History 1550–1760*. London: Edward Arnold, 1997, 39.

3. The genealogy notes in Anne Glydd's British Library ADD. 45196 are particularly interesting. She enters the birth dates of her grandchildren and reminds God if the children are able to live, they will be life-long servants of God.
4. David Henry Drake-Brockman places the marriage of William Brockman and Anne Glydd later Brockman in 1693, but the genealogy found in Anne Glydd's (Anne Glydd Brockman's mother) recipe book dates the marriage in 1692, William's birth in 1693, and James' birth in 1696.
5. Sara Mendelson and Patricia Crawford. *Women in Early Modern England 1550–1720*. Oxford, England: Clarendon Press, 1998, 125. "The bulk of the female population married in their mid-twenties."
6. C. W. Chalklin. *Seventeenth-Century Kent: A Social and Economic History*. London: Longmans, 1965, 191.
7. Keith Wrightson. *English Society 1580–1680*. New Brunswick, NJ: Rutgers University Press, 1982, 26. Wrightson cited a 15% decrease in the gentry throughout England from 1600 to 1695.
8. Chalklin. *Seventeenth-Century Kent*, 194.
9. The family crest of the Drake-Brockmans also included the Glydd family crest, not in pretense, but rather as one-quarter of the crest.
10. During the seventeenth century, Edward Haytley, the painter, was hired to paint the Brockmans on their estate. The two resulting paintings are *Temple Pond Looking towards the Rotunda and Temple Pond from the Rotunda*.
11. Roger D. Cherry. "Ethos Versus Persona." *Written Communication* 5.3 (1988): 252.
12. Lady Anne Brockman. *Age Rectified*. London: 1709, 4. [In my argument, Lady Anne Brockman has been proven the author of this text.]
13. The unmarried and childless John Locke wrote and published his child rearing advice.
14. Brockman, *Age Rectified*, 4.
15. Ibid., 5.
16. Vivian C. Fox and Martin H. Quitt. *Loving, Parenting, and Dying: The Family Cycle in England and America, Past and Present*. New York: Psychohistory Press, 1980, 252.
17. Brockman, *Age Rectified*, 6.
18. Ibid.
19. John Locke. *Some Thoughts Concerning Education (1699)*. Ed. John W. and Jean S. Yolton. Oxford, England: Clarendon Press, 1989, 105.
20. Brockman, *Age Rectified*, 7.
21. According to the responsibilities of the Kentish gentry, Sir William was J. P. Deputy-Lieutenant for Co. Kent (1689–1690) and MP for Hythe (1690–1695). Many of the papers in the Brockman Papers are legal papers from his political work.
22. Brockman, *Age Rectified*, 8.
23. Ibid., 6.
24. Locke. *Two Treatises of Government (1690)*. Cambridge University Press, 1960, 322.
25. Locke. *Some Thoughts Concerning Education (1699)*, 109.
26. Brockman. *Age Rectified*, 25.

27. Brockman. *Age Rectified*, 10.
28. Locke. *Two Treatises of Government (1690)*, 330.
29. Locke. *Some Thoughts Concerning Education (1699)*, 160.
30. Brockman, *Age Rectified*, 15.
31. Ibid., 18.
32. Ibid.
33. Laura Growing. *Common Bodies: Women, Touch and Power in 17th Century England*. New Haven, CT: Yale University Press, 2003, 7.
34. Suzanne W. Hull. *Chaste, Silent and Obedient: English Books for Women, 1475–1640*. San Marine, CA: Huntington Library, 1982, 83.
35. Brockman, *Age Rectified*, 19.
36. Ibid., 22.
37. Ibid., 12.
38. Ibid., 21.
39. Suzanne W. Hull. *Chaste, Silent and Obedient*, 36.
40. Brockman. *Age Rectified*, 26.
41. Ibid., 34.
42. Ibid., 26.
43. Ibid., 27.
44. Ibid., 28.
45. Keith Wrightson. *Earthly Necessities: Economic Lives in Early Modern Britain*. New Haven, CT: Yale University Press 2000, 278.
46. Brockman, *Age Rectified*, 19.
47. Anne Kugler. " 'I fell myself decay apace': Old Age in the Diary of Lady Sarah Cowper (1644–1720)." Ed. Lynn Bothelho and Pat Thane. *Women and Ageing in British Society Since 1500*. London: Longman, 2001, 76.
48. Brockman, *Age Rectified*, 21.
49. Ibid., 34.
50. Ibid., 19.
51. Ibid., 30.
52. L. A. Botelho, "Images of Old Age in Early Modern Cheap Print: Women, Witches, and the Poisonous Female Body." *Power & Poverty: Old Age in Pre-Industrial Past*. Ed. Susannah R.O Howay, L. A. Botelhu, and Katherine Kitleredge. WestPoint, CT: Greenwood Press, 2000, 235.
53. Brockman, *Age Rectified*, 36.

3 *Age Rectified*—The Edition

1. Keith Hammonds, "Why the Net Really Changes Everything," *American Way* (May 2002): 55. In an interview concerning his book, *Small Pieces Loosely Joined: A Unified Theory of the Web*. Perseus Books, 2002, David Weinberger commented about the effect of the Web on the ideas of the future. Although referring to the twenty-first century, this describes the effect of seventeenth-century mother's advice books on future women writers.

2. Throughout the remainder of this chapter, I will use "Age Rectified" to refer to the holograph manuscript (British Library Add. 42601) and *Age Rectified* to refer to the printed text.
3. One of the Same Sex, Age Rectified: or, some Cautionary Hints for the Rendering it less Obnoxious to Our Selves and Others. London: 1709.
4. Percy Simpson. *Proof-Reading in the Sixteenth, Seventeenth, and Eighteenth Centuries*. London: Norwood Editions, 1976.
5. While visiting Kent in 1697, Celia Fiennes visited a paper manufacture. Her description of the process is included in the book of her travels, Celia Fiennes. *The Journeys of Celia Fiennes*. Christopher Morris, ed. London: The Cresset Press, 1949.

> There are also Paper mills which dispatches paper at a quick rate; they were then marketing brown paper when I saw it; the mill is set agoing by the water and at the same tyme it pounded the rags to morter for the paper, and it beate oatmeale and hemp and ground bread together that is at the same tyme; when the substance for the paper is pounded enough they take it in a great tub and so with a frame just of the size of the sheetes of paper, make all of small wire just as I have seen fine screens to screen corne in, only this is much closer wrought, and the clap a frame of wood round the edge, and so dip it into the tub and what is too thinn runs through; then they turn this frame down on a piece of coarse woollen just of the size of the paper and so give a knock to it and it falls off, on which they clap another such a piece of woollen cloth which is ready to lay the next frame of paper, and so till they have made a large heape which they by an board on the bottom move to a press, and so lay a board on the top and so let down a great screw and weight on it, which they force together into such a narrow compass as they know so many sheetes of paper will be reduced, and this presses out all the thinner part and leaves the paper so firme as it may be taken up sheete by sheete, and laid together to be thoroughly dryed by the wind; they told me white paper was made in the same manner only they must have while woollen to put between; there is a great number of French people in this town which are employ'd in the weaving and silk winding, I meete them every night going home in great Companyes, but then some of them were employ'd in the hopping, it being the season for pulling. (124)

6. Phillip Gaskell. *A New Introduction to Bibliography*. Oxford, England: Clarendon Press, 1972, 83. "Fog. 43. A gathering of section, of three sheets of folio, quired (2? in 6s)."
7. Simpson, *Proof Reading*, 49. Simpson cites Joseph Moxon in addition to his own research with texts from the period.
8. Simpson, *Proof Reading*, 51.
9. Printers often used their own spelling system. As a research assistant for the *Hamlet Variorum* Project, the spelling preferences of individual printers has helped identify how a particular book was printed. See, Eric Rasmussen with Jennifer Forsyth, Robert Lerner, and Marsha Urban. "Blindness and

Insight: Damaged Type, Damaged Eyes, and Q2 *Hamlet*," May 4, 1998, May 6, 1998 <http://www.ardenshakespeare.com/main/ardennet/scholarship/may1998/rasmussen.html>.

10. To profit by.
11. Although many portray seventeenth-century England as a pastoral paradise when multigenerational homes flourished, the household reality for the general population consisted of the nuclear family—parents and children. The estates of the aristocracy and gentry, however, often contained a multigenerational family.
12. See John Locke. *Two Treatises of Government*. Cambridge, England: Cambridge University Press, 1960.

    Sect. 55. Their parents have a sort of rule and jurisdiction over them, when they come into the world, and for some time after; but it is but a temporary one. The bonds of this subjection are like the swaddling clothes they are wrapt up in, and support by, in the weakness of their infancy: age and reason as they grow up, loosen them, till at length they drop quite off, and leave a man at his own free disposal (322).
13. See John Locke. *Some Thoughts Concerning Education (1699)*. Ed. John W. and Jean S. Yolton. Oxford, England: Clarendon Press, 1989, 105.

    Section 37. Before they go, they Principle them with Violence, Revenge, and Cruelty. *Give me a blow that I may beat him*, is a Lesson, which most Children every Day hear: And it is thought nothing, because their Hands have not Strength to do any Mischief. But I ask, Does not this corrupt their Minds? (105)
14. What it behooves one to do; obligation, duty.
15. Only respect for superior age.
16. The Great Chain of Being is a premise that every existing thing in the universe has its "place" in the hierarchical order divinely ordained. The more spirit an object contained, the higher its place in the chain (e.g., Human beings are higher than animals). A microcosm of the universal designed social standing in society.
17. Etc.
18. Psalm 127:2 "It is vain for you to rise up early, to sit up late, to eat the bread of sorrows: for so he giveth his beloved sleep."

    Proverbs 27:14 "He that blesseth his friend with a load voice, rising early in the morning, it shall be counted a curse to him."
19. 2 Corinthians 6:14–15 "Be ye not unequally yoked together with unbelievers: for what fellowship hat righteousness with unrighteousness? and what communion hat light with darkness? And what concord hath Christ with Belial? or what part hath he that believeth with an infidel?" Belial is the spirit of evil personified; used from early times as a name for the Devil or one of his friends.
20. Relation between persons or communities, usually qualified as good, friendly, fair, ill, etc.
21. The return of an estate to the heirs or the sum that falls to be paid upon the death of a person, ex: life insurance.
22. A particular, especially a personal, need, want, or requirement.
23. Suit of clothes.

24. To imagine, fancy, think.
25. This paragraph has the same flavor as the 17th Century Nun's Prayer.
26. 1 Corinthians 9:22 "To the weak became I as weak, that I might gain the weak: I am made all things to all men, that I might save some."
27. Gaining, or by which one gains money or wealth; profitable, lucrative.
28. Intensifies, fans the fire.
29. Bald head.
30. Clothing.
31. The chief or paramount issue, the most important eventuality.
32. Thorough.
33. That which is conceived in the mind, a conception, notion, idea, thought; device.
34. One who associates with or accompanies another; a mate; a fellow.
35. Attributing something, usually a fault.
36. George Herbert. *A Church-Porch*.
37. Ally.
38. Of persons, their eyes, countenances, etc.: To frown, scowl; to look angry or sullen. Also, to be depressed or mournful. Const. at, on, upon; rarely in indirect passive.
39. Ancient, aged.
40. Pregnant.
41. Failure to observe or pay attention.
42. Changing fortune.
43. In Anne Glydd's commonbook, she tells her grandchild of her husband's philosophy for a good life, and then, much like her daughter Anne Brockman, finishes with: "Let this thing be remembered by you when my body shal be desouled into Dust."

Appendix

1. Add. 42,612, British Library, Brockman Papers.
2. Add. 42,612, British Library, Brockman Papers.
3. ADD 42587 40v.
4. ADD 45196 83r.
5. ADD 45196 83v.
6. ADD 45196 84r.

Bibliography

Abbot, Mary. *Life Cycles in England, 1560–1720: Cradle to Grave*. London: Routledge, 1996.

Advice to the women and maidens of London by one of that sex, Cornhill, England: Benjamine Billingssley, 1678.

Aughterson, Kate, ed. *Renaissance Woman: A Sourcebook: Constructions of Femininity in England*. London: Routledge, 1995.

Barstow, Anne Llewellyn. *Witchcraze: A New History of the European Witch Hunts*. New York: Pandora, 1995.

Becon, Thomas. *The Catechism*. Cambridge: University Press, 1844.

Beier, Lucinda McCray. *Sufferers & Healers: The Experience of Illness in Seventeenth-Century England*. London: Routledge & Kegan Paul, 1987.

Beilin, Elains V. *Redeeming Eve: Women Writers of the English Renaissance*. Princeton, NJ: Princeton University Press, 1987.

Bever, Edward. "Old Age and Witchcraft in Early Modern Europe." *Witchcraft, Women, and Society*. Volume 10. Ed. Brian P. Levack. New York: Garland Publishing, Inc., 1992.

Borzello, Frances. *Seeing Ourselves: Women's Self-Portraits*. London: Harry N. Abrams, Inc. Publishers, 1998.

Botelho, L. A. "Images of Old Age in Early Modern Cheap Print: Women, Witches, and the Poisonous Female Body." *Power & Poverty: Old Age in Pre-Industrial Past*. Ed. Susannah R. Ottaway, L. A. Botelho, and Katherine Kittredge. West Point, CN: Greenwood Press, 2002. 225–246.

Botelho, Lynn. "Old Age and Menopause in Rural Women of Early Modern Suffolk." Ed. Lynn Botelho and Pat Thane. *Women and Ageing in British Society Since 1500*. 43–65.

Botelho, Lynn and Pat Thane, eds. "Introduction." *Women and Ageing in British Society Since 1500*. London: Pearson Education, 2001. 1–12.

Bowers, Fredson. *On Editing Shakespeare*. Charlottesville, VA: University Press of Virginia, 1966.

Brockman, Anne. *Age Rectified*. London, 1709.

Brown, Sylvia, ed. *Women's Writing in Stuart England: The Mother's Legacies of Dorothy Leigh, Elizabeth Jocelin, and Elizabeth Richardson*. Phoenix Mill, England: Sutton Publishing Limited, 1999.

Burke, Peter. *Popular Culture in Early Modern Europe*. New York: Harper Torchbooks, 1978.

Bush, M. L. *The English Aristocracy: A Comparative Synthesis*. Manchester University Press, Manchester, England, 1984.

Chalklin, C. W. *Seventeenth-Century Kent: A Social and Economic History*. London: Longmans, 1965.

Cherry, Roger D. "Ethos Versus Persona." *Written Communication*. 5.3 (1988):252.

Clinton, Elizabeth. *The Countesse of Linclones Nurserie*. Oxford, England: John Lichfield and James Short, 1628.

Craig, Martha J. " 'Write it upon the walles of you houses': Dorothy Leigh's *The Mothers Blessing*." *Women's Life-Writing: Finding Voice/Building Community*. Ed. Linda S. Coleman. Bowling Green, OH: Bowling Green State University Popular Press, 1997. 191–208.

Crawford, Patricia. "The Construction and Experience of Maternity in Seventeenth-Century England." Ed. Valerie Fildes *Women as Mothers in Pre-Industrial England*. London: Routledge, 1990. 3–38.

Crawford, Patricia. "Women's published writing 1600–1700." *Women in English Society 1500–1800*. Ed. Mary Prior. New York: Methuen, 1985. 216.

Cressy, David. *Birth, Marriage, and Death: Ritual, Religion, and the Life-Cycle in Tudor and Stuart England*. Oxford, England: Oxford University Press, 1997.

D'Monté, Rebecca and Nicole Pohl, eds. *Female Communities, 1600–1800: Literary Visions and Cultural Realities*. Houndmills, England: Macmillan Press; New York: St. Martin's Press in association with the Institute of English Studies, School of Advanced Study, University of London, 2000.

DeShazer, Mary K., ed. *The Longman Anthology of Women's Literature*. New York: Longman, 2001.

Drake-Brockman, David Henry. *Record of the Brockman and Drake-Brockman Family*. Lindfield, Sussex, England: D. H. Drake-Brockman, 1936.

Eisenstein, Elizabeth L. *The Printing Revolution in Early Modern Europe*. Cambridge, England: Cambridge Universiy Press, 1983.

Ezell, Margaret J. M. *The Patriarch's Wife: Literary Evidence and the History of the Family*. Chapel Hill, NC: University of North Carolina Press, 1987.

Ezell, Margaret J. M. *Writing Women's Literary History*. Baltimore, MD: Johns Hopkins University Press, 1993.

Fesserson, Susanna. *A Bargain for Bachelors Or: The Best Wife In the World for Penny*. E. A., 1675.

Finlay, Roger. *Population and Metropolis: the Demography of London, 1580–1650*. Cambridge, England: Cambridge University Press, 1981.

Fox, Vivian C. and Martin H. Quitt, *Loving, Parenting, and Dying: The Family Cycle in England and America, Past and Present*. New York: Psychohistory Press, 1980.

Fraser, Antonia. *The Weaker Vessel*. New York: Alfred A. Knopf, 1984.

Fumerton, Patricia and Simon Hunt, Eds. *Renaissance Culture and the Everyday*. Philadelphia: University of Pennsylvania Press, 1999.

Gaskell, Phillip. *A New Introduction to Bibliography*. Oxford, England: Clarendon Press, 1972.

Goreau, Angeline. *The Whole Duty of a Woman: Female Writers in Seventeenth-Century England*. New York: Doubleday & Co., Inc., 1985.

Greetham, D. C. *Textual Scholarship: An Introduction.* New York: Garland Publishing, Inc., 1992.

Greetham, D. C., ed. *Scholarly Editing: A Guide to Research.* New York: The Modern Language Association of America, 1995.

Growing, Laura. *Common Bodies: Women, Touch & Power in 17th Century England.* New Haven, CT: Yale University Press, 2003.

Grundy, Isobel and Susan Wiseman, eds. *Women, Writing, History 1640–1740.* Athens, Georgia: University of Georgia Press, 1992.

Grymeston, Elizabeth, *Miscelanea, Meditatins, Memoratiues.* London, 1604.

Guillemeau, Jacques. *Child-Birth, or the Happy Deliverie of Women.* London, 1622; STC 12496, 1616.

Habermas, Jürgen. *The Structural Transformation of the Public Sphere: An Inquiry into a Category of Bourgeois Society.* Translated by Thomas Burger with the assistance of Frederick Lawrence. Cambridge, MA: MIT Press, 1989.

Hobby, Elaine. "Skills Books—Housewifery, Medicine, Midwifery." Chapter 7. *Virtue of Necessity: English Women's Writing 1649–88.* Ann Arbor, MI: University of Michigan Press, 1992.

Houlbrooke, Ralph. *The English Family: 1450–1700.* London: Longman, 1984.

Houlbrooke, Ralph. *English Family Life, 1576–1716: An Anthology from Diaries.* New York: Basil Blackwell, 1989.

Hudson, Roger, ed. *The Grand Quarrel: Women's Memoirs of the English Civil War.* Gloucestershire, England: Sutton Publishing, 1993.

Hull, Suzanne W. *Chaste, Silent & Obedient: English Books for Women, 1475–1640.* San Marino, CA: Huntington Library, 1982.

Hull, Suzanne W. *Women According to Men: The World of Tudor-Stuart Women.* London: AltaMira Press, 1996.

Josceline, Elizabeth. *The Mothers Legacy to her Unborn Childe.* Ed. Jean LeDrew Metcalfe. Toronto: Universiy of Toronto Press, 2000.

Jones, Ann Rosalind. "Surprising Fame: Renaissance Gender Ideologies and Women's Lyric." *The Poetics of Gender.* Ed. Nancy K. Miller. New York: Columbia University Press, 1986.

Jinner, Sarah. *Almanack*, London: J. S., 1659.

John, Judith Gero. "Commands and Whispers: Renaissance Parental Advice Books, Their Tradition, and Their Value in Literary Studies." Diss. Kansas State University, 1993.

Keeble, N. H., ed. *The Cultural Identity of Seventeenth-century Woman: A Reader.* New York: Routledge, 1994.

Kertzer, David I. and Peter Laslett. *Aging in the Past: Demography, Society, and Old Age.* Berkeley: University of California Press, 1995.

King, Gregory. *Natural and Political Observations.* (1696).

Kintgen, Eugene R. "Introduction." *Reading in Tudor England.* Pittsburgh, PA: University of Pittsburgh Press, 1996.

Kugler, Anne. " 'I feel myself decay apace': Old Age in the diary of Lady Sarah Cowper (1644–1720)." Ed. Lynn Botelho and Pat Thane. *Women and Ageing in British Society Since 1500.* 66–88.

Laslett, Peter, ed. *Household and Family in Past Time.* Cambridge, England: Cambridge University Press, 1972.

Laslett, Peter. *The World We Have Lost*. 2nd ed. 1965. New York: Charles Scribner's Sons, 1973.

Leigh, Dorothy. *The Mothers Blessing or The godly counsail of a Gentle-woman not long since deceases, left behind for her Children*. London: John Pudge, 1616.

Lerner, Gerda. *The Creation of Feminist Consciousness: From the Middle Ages to Eighteen-seventy*. Oxford: Oxford University Press, 1993.

Lewalski, Barbara Kiefer. *Writing Women in Jacobean England*. Cambridge, MA.: Harvard University Press, 1993.

Locke, John. *Two Treatises of Government*. Cambridge, England: Cambridge University Press, 1960.

Locke, John. *Some Thoughts Concerning Education (1699)*. Ed. John W. and Jean S. Yolton. Oxford, England: Clarendon Press, 1989.

Love, Harold. "Scribal Publication in 17th-Century England." *Transactions of the Cambridge Bibliographical Society*. 9 (1987):130–154.

McGann, Jerome J. *The Textual Condition*. Princeton, NJ: Princeton University Press, 1991.

McLaren, Dorothy. "Fertility, Infant Mortality, and Breast Feeding in the Seventeenth Century." *Medical History*. 22 (1978):378–396.

McLaren, Dorothy, "Marital Fertility and Lactation 1570–1720." *Women in English Society 1500–1800*. Ed. Mary Prior. London: Methuen, 1985.

Macfarlane, Alan. *Marriage and Love in England: Modes of Reproduction 1300–1840*. Oxford, England: Basil Blackwell, 1986.

Maclean, Ian. *The Renaissance Notion of Woman: A Study in the Fortunes of Scholasticism and Medical Science in European Intellectual Life*. Cambridge, England: Cambridge University Press, 1980.

Martin, Randall, ed. *Women Writers in Renaissance England*. London: Longman, 1997.

Mendelson, Sara and Patricia Crawford. *Women in Early Modern England 1550–1720*. Oxford: Clarendon Press, 1998.

Metcalfe, Jean LeDrew, ed. "The Introduction." *The Mothers Legacy to her Unborn Childe*. Toronto: University of Toronto Press, 2000.

Mills, Sara. *Discourse*. London: Routledge, 1997.

One of the Same Sex. *Age Rectified: or, some Cautionary Hints for the Rendering it less Obnoxious to Our Selves and Others*. London: 1709.

Otten, Charlotte F., ed. "General Introduction." *English Women's Voices 1540–1700*. Miami, FL: Florida International University Press, 1992.

Plant, Marhorie. *The English Book Trade: An Economic History of the Making and Sale of Books*. London: George Allen & Unwin Ltd., 1974 (1939).

Pollock, Adrian. "Social and Economic Characteristics of Witchcraft Accusations in Sixteenth- and Seventeenth-Century Kent." *Witchcraft, Women, and Society*. Volume 10. Ed. Brian P. Levack. 197–208.

Prior, Mary, ed. *Women in English Society 1500–1800*. London: Methuen, 1995.

Reay, Barry. *Popular Cultures in England 1550–1750*. Essex, England: Addison Wesley Longman Limited, 1998.

Richardson, Elizabeth. *A Ladies Legacy to her Daughters*. Ed. Charlotte F. Otten. Miami, FL: Florida International University Press, 1992.

Rochschild, Arlie Russell. "The Commercial Spirit of Intimate Life and the Abduction of Feminism: Signs from Women's Advice Books." *Theory, Culture & Society*. 11, 2 (May 1994):1–24.

Schleiner, Louise. *Tudor and Stuart Women Writers*. Bloomington, IN: Indiana University Press, 1994.

Schofield, Roger. "Did the Mothers Really Die? Three Centuries of Maternal Mortality in 'The World We Have Lost.' " *The World We Have Gained*. Ed. Lloyd Bonfield, Richard M. Smith, and Keith Wrightson. Oxford, London, Oxford University Press, 1986. 231–260.

Sharpe, J. A. *Early Modern England: A Social History 1550–1760*. London: Edward Arnold, 1987.

Sizemore, Christine W. "Early Seventeenth-Century Advice Books: The Female Viewpoint." *South Atlantic Bulletin*. 41.1 (1976):41–48.

Sizemore, Christine W. "Attitudes Toward the Education Roles of Women: Sixteenth-Century Advice Books." *The University of Dayton Review*. 15.1 (1981): 57–67.

Simpson, Percy. *Proof-Reading in the Sixteenth, Seventeenth, and Eighteenth Centuries*. London: Norwood Editions, 1976 (1935).

Stone, Lawrence. *The Family, Sex and Marriage in England, 1500–1800*. New York: Harper & Row, 1977.

Tanselle, G. Thomas. *A Rationale of Textual Criticism*. Philadelphia, PA: University of Pennsylvania Press, 1992.

Tebeaux, Elizabeth. "Technical Writing for Women of the English Renaissance: Technology, Literacy, and the Emergence of a Genre." *Written Communication*. 10.2: (1993) 164–199.

Tebeaux, Elizabeth and Mary M. Lay. "The Emergence of the Feminine Voice, 1526–1640: The Earliest Published Books by English Renaissance Women." *Journal of Composition Theory*. 1995. 15.1 (1995):53–81.

Travitsky, Betty, ed. *The Paradise of Women: Writings by Englishwomen of the Renaissance*. New York: Columbia University Press, 1989.

Travitsky, Betty S. and Adele F. Seeff, eds. *Attending to Women in Early Modern England*. London: Associated University Presses, 1994.

Trill, Suzanne, Kate Chedgzoy, and Melanie Osborne, eds. *Lay by Your Needles Ladies, Take the Pen: Writing Women in England, 1500–1700*. London: Arnold, 1997.

Wayne, Valerie. "Advice for Women from Mothers and Patriarchs." Chapter 3. *Women and Literature in Britain, 1500–1700*. Ed. Helen Wilcox. Cambridge: Cambridge University Press, 1998. 56–79.

Wiesner, Merry E. *Women and Gender in Early Modern Europe*. 2nd ed. Cambridge, England: Cambridge University Press, 2000.

Wilcox, Helen. *Women and Literature in Britain, 1500–1700*. Cambridge, England: Cambridge University Press, 1996.

Wrigley, Edward and Roger Schofield. *The Population History of England 1541–1871: A Reconstruction*. Cambridge, MA: Harvard University Press, 1981.

Wrightson, Keith. *English Society 1580–1680*. New Brunswick, NJ: Rutgers University Press, 1982.

Wrightson, Keith. *Earthly Necessities; Economic Lives in Early Modern Britain*. New Haven, CT: Yale University Press, 2000.

Woolf, Virginia. *A Room of One's Own*. 1929. New York: Harcourt Brace & Company, 1989.

Woodbridge, Linda. *Women and the English Renaissance: Literature and the Nature of Womankind, 1540–1620*. Chicago: University of Illinois Press, 1984.

Index